A Life Outdoors

A Life Outdoors

A Curmudgeon Looks at the Natural World

WAYNE HANLEY

The Massachusetts Audubon Society

DRAWINGS BY MICHAEL A. DIGIORGIO

THE STEPHEN GREENE PRESS / Brattleboro, Vermont

A Life Outdoors is the 1980 volume of the Man and Nature series of the Massachusetts Audubon Society, Lincoln, Massachusetts 01773.

This book has been produced in the United States of America.
It is designed by David Ford and published by The Stephen Greene Press, Fessenden Road, Brattleboro, Vermont 05301.

Library of Congress Cataloging in Publication Data

Hanley, Wayne, 1915–
  A life outdoors.

  (Man and nature; 1980)
  1. Natural history—New England—Addresses,
essays, lectures.   2. Outdoor life—New England—
Addresses, essays, lectures.   3. Hanley, Wayne,
1915– —Addresses, essays, lectures.
4. Naturalists—United States—Biography—Addresses, essays, lectures.   I. Title.   II. Series:
Man and nature (Lincoln, Mass.); 1980.

| QH1.M27 | 1980 | [QH104.5.N4] | 304.2s | [574.974] | 80–21980 |

ISBN 0–8289–0403–0 (pbk.)
ISBN 0–8289–0402–2 (Mass. Audubon Society pbk.)

Contents

Foreword by Paul Brooks   vii

Preface   ix

JANUARY
White Paper Tree   1
Rolled in Winter's Grip   3
The Glorious Flexible Flyer   5
Owner of a Second Home   7

FEBRUARY
In Praise of White Pine   10
Swish of Snowshoes   12
Disappearing Night Trill   14
Love and the Great Horned Owl   16

MARCH
Fastest Gun in the East   20
Spring Night Twitter   21
Lucky 13   24
Beat It, Kid   27

APRIL
Little Mud-Smearer   30
Too Much Credit to Kentucky   32
When You Know You're Right   34
Loneliness   36

MAY
The Loping Screamer   40
Gathering Bracken Seed   43
Poets' Bird   45
Popping Like Ping-Pong Balls   47

JUNE

Homing in on Humans   50

Awakened by an Oriole   51

Farewell to a Falcon   54

A Holdover Dragon   56

JULY

Missing the Mark on Moles   59

Thoreau's Night Warbler   62

Henny Penny Remembered   64

Yankee Character Defect   66

AUGUST

Gangly, but Bluest of Blue   69

The Snake Doctor   71

Susan, Beloved, Who Were You?   73

Poor Guards for Hen Houses   75

SEPTEMBER

A Bonus with Tomatoes   78

Huge Black Eyes   80

The Air Restored   82

Never Twice the Same   84

OCTOBER

The Vine-Grown Lantern   87

Prejudice and Geese   89

The Non-Conforming Woodchuck   91

What Is a Forest?   94

NOVEMBER

Giving Spiders Work   96

Living with Crows   98

Eternal Spiny Welcome   101

Flight from Darkness   103

DECEMBER

Builders of Stately Mansions   106

The Breathing Rivers   108

Tooting down Trunks   109

Is Holly Hex Still Potent?   111

EPILOGUE

Surviving Survival Training   114

Foreword

Paul Brooks

Though I am sure that he does not think of himself in such lofty terms, Wayne Hanley is a modern representative of a great tradition: that of the articulate naturalist. A large part of his life has been devoted to the enjoyable though demanding task of interpreting the world of nature to the general public. In so doing he has helped to create the sense of awareness, the simple delight in the out-of-doors, which is an essential aspect of today's so-called environmental movement.

As Henry Thoreau remarked, the important thing is not what you look at, but what you see. Wayne Hanley taught himself to see as a young boy roaming the countryside of northwest Missouri. In college he started out as a premedical student, enraptured by the study of biology, zoology, botany, and chemistry. Later, in the financial squeeze of the Great Depression, he switched to the more immediately productive profession of journalism. Obviously he hadn't planned it that way, but the fusion of these two interests created the perfect background for his future career. As a reporter in the Midwest he began writing nature columns and feature articles on wildlife. From 1964 to 1980 he was editor of publications for the Massachusetts Audubon Society and wrote a weekly column for the Society, which was distributed to newspapers and radio stations throughout New England. Some of these essays are published here in lasting form.

Foreword

Both figuratively and literally, Wayne's writing is down to earth. In a casual manner, often drily humorous, he manages to convey masses of information without ever seeming to teach. Why are mosquitoes fiercest at dawn and dusk? How is bracken associated with witchcraft? Whence the name "daisy" and why the cone-shaped "eye" of the black-eyed Susan? What are you really doing when you dam a brook? Where did our red foxes come from, and why are gray foxes no good for hunting with hounds? More important, whence comes most of the oxygen we breathe? The facts are here—and a philosophy of life as well. Wayne does not rate all change as progress. He prefers the snowshoe to the snowmobile.

He is, in fact, particularly fond of snowshoeing. "I am a northern person," he writes. Apparently he rejoices in the cold. In short, a cryophile. ("When you call me that, smile!") For him the winterless climate of the tropics has no allure.

A field observer, Wayne is equally at home in the stacks of a library. Here he ferrets out forgotten treasures, such as the writings of the early naturalists which he presented so learnedly in his recent book, *Natural History in America*. May he have ample time in the future for projects as rewarding as that one and as the present volume of essays.

Preface

How did I get here?

The "here" is the office of editor of publications for the Massachusetts Audubon Society. For more than sixteen years I have been filling a position which earlier I had considered an excellent post for a maypole dancer. But on a formal greensward, I'm a stumble-bum. It has to be wild and natural or it does not interest me.

Actually, my route to this chair has been marked by anger. Sometimes anger that makes the neck arteries bulge with hot blood. The sort of anger that one must cool, lest the gods leave one open to destruction. It involves the unfairness of supposedly intelligent man and his dealings with lesser-favored creatures, and with the environment that supports us all—human, beast, and plant. You will not find that anger stated so crudely again in this book. I hope, instead, that as you read the natural history sections of the volume your own sense of justice toward nature will be buttressed.

But, enough of that! What follows is a string of brief and, I hope, interesting discussions taken from the 800-plus columns that I have written for the Massachusetts Audubon Society and the Audubon Society of Rhode Island. Sprinkled among them for a change of pace are several autobiographical sketches. Since I remember the events recounted in them, they must have influenced my life. It is unfortunate that I cannot tell you how.

I can assure you that all the influences upon my life are not here. Missing in this recounting is the name Eleanor,

Preface

borne by that girl who still looks to me much as she did forty-four years ago when we were married, while still in college and in the midst of the historic Depression. She is a journalist, too, and well able to type for herself if ever she is of a mind to admit you to our privacy. Nor do I mention, except in this sentence, a daughter who is a botanist, science teacher, mother, and writer.

My saga began long ago in Leavenworth, Kansas, where my mother, who was the daughter of a railroad conductor, married my father, who was a railroad brakeman. The scene quickly switched to Trenton, Missouri, a railroad center for the Rock Island Railroad. My father had acquired enough seniority to bump his way to a job back in Trenton, where he had started out on the rail career. I was born in Trenton. Details appear elsewhere in this volume.

After the usual pains caused by my skeleton growing faster than my muscles, I reached that age when I was ashamed to be seen with my parents. In other words, my development was fairly normal. I was a newsboy while going through the aging process. It taught me several skills, like smoking cigarettes at the age of nine and, soon after, learning to drink bootleg moonshine or thumbed beer. Thumbed beer was a Prohibition specialty. One uncapped a bottle of a nauseous substance known as near beer, poured grain alcohol into the bottle until the neck was filled. The alcohol smoothed out the taste. I was an only child and had only the neighborhood children to teach me. I was precocious, if nothing else.

I spent so much time bumming around our few wooded hills, wandering along the railroad right of way, and musing at a local marsh known as The Quarter Stretch, that that sort of life seemed natural to me. So much so that I really did not miss these outdoor contacts with basic reality until I finished college and went to work as a reporter on the *Kansas City Star*. City life was different.

After undistinguished service as an infantryman in World War II, I returned to Kansas City. Fortunately, the housing shortage forced us to live at the perimeter of the city. The rural apartment was within walking distance of the Blue River. I made the trip to the river each morning. I could stay until 11:00 A.M. I worked on the morning edition of *The Star*, which meant my hours were from 2:00 P.M. to 11:30 P.M. It was a poor arrangement for anyone who wished to be a social lion. But it was ideal for a naturalist.

In 1950 my family moved to Boston because my wife came from a Rhode Island–New Hampshire family and she missed New England. Once again I was working afternoon and night hours on a newspaper, this time in a region which is a naturalist's paradise. For more than ten years I spent every morning through every season roaming a large natural area in Hingham. There was something new to be seen every day. That is, if one were knowledgeable enough to recognize the gentle foldings and unfoldings of the seasons.

With that background, I seized without question the opportunity to go to work for the Massachusetts Audubon Society.

My earliest memory involves my mother with a Montgomery Ward catalogue under her right arm and me clutched by her left hand. I was three years old, going on four. We were walking to the barn. There was a horse in that barn. It was a paint pony, a white creature that looked as though browns and blacks and tans had been splashed on it from paint pots. My mother was a city woman, reared in rural metropolises of up to three thousand residents. She had acquired cabin fever. She and I lived out in the country about three miles from my grandmother's house. My father was a railroad freight train brakeman, away from home days at a time. My mother had had enough of loneliness. My father had not shown her how to harness the horse. So she took the Montgomery Ward catalogue to the barn, propped it on a feedbox, and draped the leather over the horse in accordance with the pictures advertising harness. As did so many of her do-it-yourself projects, the harness caper succeeded.

Getting on with the paint pony and buggy; the combination shaped my early life in two ways. One day as my mother drove up the steep incline of dirt road that lifted

Preface

buggies and wagons up to the single-track crossing of the OK Railroad right-of-way, the pony saw something over the top of this hump that we did not see. It was a girl in a white dress with huge dark polka dots. The sight was enough to spook the horse. It took off at a wild gallop. The buggy was catapulted into the air, like one of those pursued automobiles on modern television. My mother and I sailed clear of the buggy. Mother landed on top of me in the dirt. She always said she did it to protect me. I always suspected it just came out that way.

My other learning experience in the buggy concerned a tin of sugar wafers. Sugar wafers were sold in airtight, flat tins in those days. Bakers had the idea that customers wanted the product fresh, pure, and uncrumbled. Mother was eating the sugar wafers and offered me one. She took it out of the tin and poked it toward me. I demanded the privilege of picking my own wafer from the tin. Mother said the tin was dangerous. I was adamant and crying. She was adamant and eating. It was a great lesson. I learned how quickly an adult can eat an entire tin of sugar wafers.

But let us now get on with the experiences in natural history which make up the more valuable passages of this volume.

Jan.

White Paper Tree

January is the month of the birches, and the most beautiful is the paper birch.

The paper birch likes to be where glaciers have been. It thrives where the soil has been bulldozed by the shearing, cutting edge of the great ice faces that scraped across New England. When the glaciers retreated, the paper birch chased the melting ice right back up to the northern timber line.

If one seeks the paper birch in southern New England, one had best look to the northern or eastern exposure on hills. For the paper birch has failed to make peace with the sun. Any acreage where the July temperature exceeds an average of seventy degrees must settle for less than the paper birch. It might attract the yellow birch which gropes down the Appalachians as far as northern Alabama. But the paper birch remains a northern elite.

Should anything prettier than the white on white of a paper birch standing erect in the snow occur, postcard photographers undoubtedly would capitalize upon it. Since they seem to have found nothing that surpasses the birch, perhaps we should accept it as the northland standard for boreal beauty.

The paper birch was the canoe birch of the northern Indians. In as much as we now have aluminum, let us leave the paper birch bark where it belongs, wrapped around a birch trunk. Removal of bark can kill the birch tree—indeed, definitely kills it if the tree is girdled. In any event, the removal of bark leaves a black scar where white should be.

1

One could be excused for a selfish attitude toward the birch. But we in the Western Hemisphere are not alone in admiring it. The birch genus (*Betula*) has at least forty species scattered around the northern polar region. Birches similar to ours occur in Europe, the Himalayas, and down into mainland China.

Birches, of course, do more than stand there and look nice. They are active in community affairs. Birch catkins, buds and seeds are a good food source for ruffed grouse. Other birds and animals that utilize birch or birch products include chickadees, purple finches, redpolls, pine siskins, beaver, snowshoe hare, porcupine, deer, and moose.

Rolled in Winter's Grip

On bitter cold nights when a deep breath causes the lungs to burn as though touched by flame, the evergreen rhododendrons droop their leathery leaves and roll them like so many panatella cigars of good green Havana leaf.

This is the season when the broad-leaved evergreens stand the test that other shrubs avoided by turning their leaves to gold or red and dropping them on an autumn breeze. Into his crucible King Boreas dumps acid sharpness of below-zero temperatures and stirs with a drying Arctic wind. The wind-blown snow rattles against these leaves that hang dejected, appearing as lifeless as the poinsettia leaves that dry on a withering plant in a nearby window.

Let winter break its grip for an instant and relax into a January thaw, and the rhododendrons unroll those leaves and give them a freshness of spring.

It is a mystery of nature why some plants brave a northern winter with their leaves intact, while others of the same family dodge the issue by shedding theirs. There are, of

course, advantages to keeping leaves. It is an ancient legacy that the pines and spruces have kept bright since eons before our more familiar deciduous trees developed broad leaves that drop each autumn.

By keeping the leaves it already has, such shrubs as rhododendrons save themselves the energy of growing a new canopy each spring. All they need do is unfurl their old leaves to the sun and devote the new energy of spring to growing new growth above the old.

But, to accomplish the conservation of energy, the broad-leaved evergreens need especially efficient leaves. They are tough leaves that resist the loss of moisture that more ordinary leaves spend so lavishly in summer. The broad-leaved evergreens furl their leaves to close the underside "pores" that leak water to the dry winds of winter. They must conserve water, since water is necessary to life, and when the ground is frozen there is too little free water for the roots to take up.

The rhododendrons' cousins, the azaleas, chose instead to drop their leaves. There are hollies that have lost Yule spirit and shed leaves in autumn along with the maples.

One hardly ever hears of Charlie Ross anymore.

When I was four years old, mention of Charlie's name would make my eyes bug with fear. Charlie had disappeared, back in Philadelphia, or some place like that. Or so we children understood. Any place east of the Grundy County limits was foreign soil to us. Just as was anything north, south, or west. And that included the remainder of Missouri as well as places like nearby Iowa. So Charlie had disappeared somewhere, however vague.

What made Charlie's disappearance important was the fact that gypsies had stolen him. It was a simple age. Today police would look elsewhere for Charlie's kidnappers. But in our era only strangers would kidnap, and gypsies fit the bill.

It was because of Charlie that my mother would dash into the yard and shoo me inside the house when gypsies

*passed our farm. It was the same farm with painted pony,
barn, and Montgomery Ward catalogue. Gypsies did pass
along the dirt road at the lane's end. They came along in
caravans of four to six covered wagons, each pulled by
four horses. One could see gypsy children in bright reds,
blues, and yellows, all bandanna-brilliant cloth. Maybe one of
them was Charlie Ross. Mother never let the gypsies land
at our place. Somewhere near the middle of the line of
wagons, the gypsies had a herd of horses. The horses were
their business. The gypsies were horse traders. People said
they were sharp dealers. They would have had to have
been to keep alive while out-trading the average backwoods
Missouri show-me character. Some people, however, believed gypsies made a living stealing goods and kidnapping
children. And not all who held that belief were four years
old.*

The Glorious Flexible Flyer

It has been an unfortunate winter for meadow mice and me.
There's been too little snow for either of us.
Probably the invasion by northern shrikes has been fueled

by meadow mice that lacked the protection of tunnels under the snow. Certainly there have been few birds around that shrikes really appreciate, with the exception of house sparrows. I am supposing that you know that shrikes are songbirds that live a bird of prey lifestyle. They pounce upon small birds and mice, knock them silly with a heavy beak, and then strip them of meat.

The things that prey upon me do not sit upon fence posts or utility wires. So snow does not help me much in avoiding the parasites. I do, however, miss snow. Bare ground in midwinter produces nostalgia so severe that it borders upon withdrawal symptoms. It all began with a Flexible Flyer sled that I found beneath a Christmas tree many seasons ago. It was a technological breakthrough, that sled. Most of the sleds in the neighborhood were handmade, from hardwood, and with bent iron rod runners. Fathers could make sleds in those days. Fathers were much bigger and more impressive than they are today.

So there I was, one of the few kids within miles who owned a store-bought sled whose steel runners were painted red. A real status symbol had appeared magically in the living room. In some ways it was my last triumph. From then on, things sort of always went downhill for me. But not with that sled; not immediately, that is. For the sled arrived on one of those years when one could look beyond the Christmas tree and see outside the window the brown, barren ground. I thought it never would snow again.

I am a northern person, and that sled may have made me so. My heroes were Cook, Peary, Amundsen, Scott—men who could hitch dogs to a sled and make polar history. As my helpmate so often has pointed out, it is a good thing that I never tried to emulate them. Anyone as basically helpless as I am would have died early on an expedition. It is an observation that one could make about almost any writer.

I remember a winter interlude misspent in southern Mexico. My companions luxuriated in the heat, to which they were unaccustomed at that season. I hung on, hoping to see a harpy eagle. I listened to the howler monkeys serenade the mountain and valley each daybreak, for I was up at dawn. I wanted to be abroad at the only time of day that the temperature was as low as seventy degrees. I missed the snow of winter. I can get the heat of the Mexican winter in our northern summers. But one never can experience the Montreal-born airconditioning of February in Mexico.

So let the snowy owls and me have our touch of snow. Give the meadow mice a protecting blanket. And when it snows, let your heart leap as though your eyes had for the first time glimpsed a Flexible Flyer sled that was all yours.

Owner of a Second Home

That bushel of dry leaves perched high in a naked tree is the second home of a gray squirrel.

In winter the squirrel nests become most evident. The green leaves that concealed them all summer long are gone. And suburban folk often mistake the massive brown bundles for hawks' nests—or, when really romanticizing, for eagle nests.

The leaf nest serves as a sort of summer camp for the gray squirrel. It is in general a rainproof and well-shaded retreat. Someplace where a squirrel can get away from it all when the whole world seems too squirrelly. It also serves as a field headquarters in an area that provides an abundant supply of nuts but too few holes to which a gray squirrel might scamper in emergencies.

In a way, the word "nest" probably should not be applied to the gray squirrel's leaf structure. A nest more properly is a haven in which the female gives birth and nurtures the young. While there are circumstances that reduce a gray squirrel to using the leaf bower as a nest, she prefers to shelter the young within a hole in a tree.

The British, who have a word for everything—but lack the good judgment that would have warned against importing gray squirrels—call the leafy bowers of gray squirrels *dreys.*

There are areas where a shortage of desirable tree holes forces gray squirrels to rely upon their own nest construction for homes and nurseries. At the edge of the Great Plains fifty years ago, gray squirrels were reduced to scurrying along telephone cables for their aerial exercise and building leaf nests between utility poles and electrical transformers. Such sites were particularly risky. Among other things, transformers in those days often were struck by lightning. A more common hazard, however, was an overlapping leaf construction that bridged two electrical cables. A thorough rain could result in electrocution of the squirrel family.

One might wonder how a squirrel family could live in an area so inhospitable that there were no mature trees which afforded sheltering holes. But, if one does, one never has farmed. For gray squirrels prefer to eat field corn rather than mess around with acorns and the like. Wherever there was corn, the squirrels had no problems beyond finding shelter.

The really durable squirrel's nest has a well-constructed floor made from twigs and sticks that have been wedged together tightly. The leaf nest begins with the construction of the platform. After sufficient leaves and twigs have been shaped into a nest, the squirrel brings shredded bark, moss, or dry grass to finish off a cavity within the structure where the animal intends relaxing.

The squirrel's leaf nest is an active world for more than squirrels. One researcher who analyzed general aspects of the gray squirrel's ecosystem found that nests in a survey area were hosts to sixty-five species of insects, thirty-two species of mites and ticks, four species of spiders, and two species of centipedes.

Possibly most persons do not realize that the ordinary rooster has huge, sharp spurs on the backs of his legs.

For those even farther removed from the scene, a rooster is a gentleman chicken.

At the age of five I had custodial duties for the meanest gang of chickens you ever saw. The hens always were trying to embarrass me by darting between my legs and out the open hen house door to freedom. But worst of all was the rooster. The rooster and I seemed about the same size, although I outweighed him. The weight differential did not dishearten that feathered beast. He saw me as an interloper. The moment I got inside the hen house, the rooster would come hurtling along the hen house floor, looking like a feathered bowling ball aimed directly at me. If I failed to get the feed can down to ankle level in time, the rooster would give me a few bloody scratches from his spurs.

In fact, tending to those chickens was the second most disgusting duty that I had. The list was topped by my having each morning to take out to the backhouse and empty the so-called slop jar (china pot), which was kept beneath my parents' bed.

Feb.

In Praise of White Pine

Only an outlander can appreciate the white pine.

New Englanders live too much among them. We take the white pine as commonplace. So much so that we find it hard to believe that the white pine was once the world's most valuable tree.

Some of this casual acceptance comes from the fact that what we see today are but remnants of the once great white pine forest. Our hills are clothed with midgets. There is no white pine alive today—let alone a white pine forest—that can convey to us a fraction of the impression the original white pine forest made upon the first white men to reach North America.

None but foresters know that the white pine can achieve the lordly might of the giant redwood. For there are no specimens left that can give an idea of what the early pine forests contained.

The white pine 150 feet tall was not an unusual tree in precolonial days. One specimen on what now is the campus of Dartmouth College in Hanover, New Hampshire, reputedly measured 240 feet tall. There were stands of white pines whose lowest branches were eighty feet above the woodland floor.

Colonial land inspectors originated the saying that a squirrel could spend its lifetime running through the white pine canopy and never touch its feet to earth. The statement was almost true, for between New England and the Great Lakes an almost continuous white pine forest existed.

The white pine seems always to have been an essentially northern tree. In a warmer era when our present Arctic

wasteland was more responsive to the sun, the white pine must have grown far north of its present Canadian limits. It must have been circumpolar to account for its present distribution and its near relatives. For our white pine relates closely to the western white pine of the United States, the Himalayan white pine of mid-Asia and the Balkan pine of Yugoslavia and Greece.

The Age of Glaciers must have pushed the pine forests deeply down the land masses of North America, Europe, and Asia. Once separated by mountain ranges and oceans, these species of white pine developed idiosyncracies that set them apart. But not so far apart that these species cannot be hybridized today.

Perhaps these pine species would have drifted farther apart on the botanical scale, except that pines were ancient and settled in their ways for eons before the only glaciers of which we have record were born. For the family of pines rank among the aristocracy of treedom. The maples and other deciduous trees that shed their leaves are Johnnies-come-lately, despite the eons that they have shaded the world.

Pines and other conifers belong to a group known as Gymnosperms, or "naked seed" plants. They were in business before nature devised a scheme of coating seeds with jackets. Indeed, the conifers were, and still are, so successful that one wonders why nature evolved seed coats.

The fact that white pines stretched an almost continuous canopy over the northeast implies that before the land was disturbed, the white pine had a hardihood even exceeding its present robustness. Such a compact crown of any organism, from grass to man, is an invitation for diseases and blights that only the most physically fit can withstand.

Swish of Snowshoes

Snowshoes can be a passport to solitude.

Since neither propelling motors nor chair lifts become involved in snowshoeing, the snowshoer requires neither a gasoline can nor a mountainside corporation to set him in motion.

He does become the victim of shortages, however. And how well the snowshoeing progresses in winter depends upon where you live. For there is no snowshoeing where there is no snow. The only exception that comes to mind concerns the north country snowshoe band that so often kicks its syncopated racquets along Washington's dry streets at inaugurals, etc.

It is fundamental to snowshoeing these days to get into the woods as quickly as possible. Otherwise, one faces a barrage of questions from bystanders. The quick escape is not as easy as it sounds. Fastening the snowshoe harness over the boot can be a time-consuming operation. Indeed, for the beginner, harnessing requires so much time that one fears the snow may melt before the last strap is buckled.

Since I wear bearpaw snowshoes, the commonest question I must answer is "Why don't your snowshoes have tails?" Bearpaws are broad snowshoes that are rounded in back, rather than trailing behind the elongation of wood that characterizes other snowshoe shapes. Bearpaws can be handled easier in the woods. One even can walk backwards on them if necessary. But the real reason I wear bearpaws is the same that accounts for most other things that all of us do; we started out that way.

On snowshoes one neither slips nor slides, or at least not by design. Instead one does what comes naturally, walks. There is nothing to learn about locomotion on snowshoes.

February

One just walks, rather normally, although it is wise to lift the foot higher when stepping. In other words, you cannot shuffle along. Especially if there is a crust on the snow. With each step, the snowshoe breaks through the crust and one must lift the racquet from that brittle trap or trip.

A physical ed teacher used to impress upon the class that if schools really were concerned about the future of the student, rather than game gate receipts, the course would concentrate upon tennis. If you own a tennis racquet and tennis skill, you need find only one other person for a game. In most parts of the world, that is possible.

But, the snowshoe racquet has the tennis racquet beat— in the northern winter at least. For one need find nothing beyond a stir in his own soul to launch a snowshoe contest against snow.

While it is possible to find a few kindred souls and stamp a highway through the woods, the quietude of solitary exploration ranks rather high among snowshoers. Surely in a world where one encounters others at almost all times, there is no antisocial content in the desire to go it alone occasionally. Nothing excels snowshoes in providing such escape.

Snowshoes are silent. When the snow is deep, one is unlikely to meet anyone in the woods. The landscape usually looks like a Christmas card. Occasionally one comes upon a fox or flushes a ruffed grouse, but not often. It would be nice to report that on snowshoes one catches glimpses of wildlife in a rare atmosphere. But, in general, that is not true. When snow is deep, animals hole up, just as people cling to a fireside.

When I was five years old my family moved back into Trenton. Missouri, that is. I had been born there. Not in the house which my father bought for the return to city life. I was born in my grandmother's house. It was common in those days to be born in your grandmother's house. There was a hospital, but no one ever went there unless they were near death. So it was assumed that if you entered the hospital, you never would come out standing erect. Anyhow, I was born at grandma's. People then were

*more accustomed to real messes in their houses than mod-
ern folks are.*

*I cost five dollars. The doctor's fee, that is. For years
they joked that I was not worth it. The doctor who delivered me had been in trouble recently. The body of a baby
had been found in the town. Its birth had not been reported. Well, the sheriff winnowed clues down to where he
thought he ought to talk to the doctor. The word got out,
somehow, and the doctor suddenly was not apparent. He
was found a few days later hiding in a haymow and pre-
tending that he was trying to eat yellow dent corn off the
cob. Of course a horse or hog has trouble trying to eat mature yellow dent corn off a cob. A man would have as good
luck biting a stone. Everybody knew that, including Doc.
So everybody sort of winked and said Doc was putting on
a good act. The nub of the matter was that Doc was a
good doctor, and the town needed him. So nothing happened to him. The sheriff more or less told him to go home
and quit that eating-corn act.*

*But who knows? Maybe my family had him deliver me
under the assumption that if I proved defective they would
not have to accept me.*

Disappearing Night Trill

The wavering trill of a screech owl on a recent evening
reminded me that I seldom hear this once common bird.

What has happened to these chubby little owls seems a
mystery. There is a dearth of material about screech owls in
the literature dealing with the decline of birds. Most likely
they have been caught between two trends: the neatness of
suburbia which disposes of dead hole-nesting trees, and a
possible decline in large beetles and other night-flying insects due to pesticide use.

One occasionally sees a screech owl hawking insects near
a street light. The most recent night-flying owl which I saw
was a screech owl seizing insects near the high-pole lights
that illuminate part of Ocean Park beach in Maine. Its

general conformation reminded me of a woodcock, but its erratic pursuit of dodging insects suggested a slow bat.

Screech owls probably would be more common near street lights, except for the danger involved. These small owls frequently become the prey of larger owls, particularly the great horned owl. Their best defense is to remain inconspicuous.

One seldom thinks of such a small bundle of feathers as fierce. Yet the screech owl becomes quite belligerent when its young are involved. At an apartment complex where I once lived, one of the more enterprising neighbors scooped up four infant screech owls which he found roosting on a low limb among the few trees that the developer had spared to make it a "garden development." He took the little birds into his apartment. The young owls disliked life in a huge brick cavity and frequently gave a thin wavering call. The result was that their parents swooped down on anyone entering or leaving the apartment house entrance. They knocked off hats and raked a few bare foreheads with their talons.

The owl-napper assumed a heroic role by shooting the two enraged adult owls. Fortunately a newspaperman lived in the garden complex and wrote up the heroic act. As a result, the owl-napper was arrested and became the neighborhood bum. Not because of what he had done, but because all his neighbors were summoned as witnesses and had to lose a day's work in going to court.

Screech owls exist in two color phases, red or gray. Red owls and gray owls often mate, and a brood may include both color phases. While it is difficult to obtain convincing evidence, the speculation is that the gray phase screech owl is much more common than the red phase, at least in most areas. Some observers say that the gray phase is replacing the red phase in areas where coniferous forests are replacing deciduous forests.

Since screech owls frequently fly in front of automobiles at night, or sometimes slam against the side of a passing car, there have been occasional censuses of the birds along highways. In some regions, among dead owls along the road, the gray phase outnumbers the red phase three-to-one. Oddly, the few screech owls I have found beside roads all have been red.

Love and the Great Horned Owl

A great horned owl has spread an aura of love over a nearby hillside.

Smitten by Cupid in mid-January, the owl has ignited a flickering flame of vernal rapture in a pair of captive great

horned owls. Perhaps it was the female of the captive pair that caused the wild owl to choose a hooting perch near the cage. Whatever the genesis of the affair, the sequence that changed the captive pair from mute to hoot required two weeks of nightly courting on the part of the wild owl. Now the repertoire of the soloist has been merged into a trio. The woods ring with melodic counterpoint.

If it seems early for birds to be courting, it is only because one has been misled by such fainthearted creatures as thrushes and warblers. The great horned owl has an ardor that cannot be cooled by below-zero temperatures. He and she accept snowdrifts and ice crusts as the trappings of a honeymoon. To them a delay until Valentine's Day would be unthinkable. It is much too late in the year for an emotion as serious as love.

One might suppose that the owls hope to build an early nest and get on with life's more rewarding aspects. But the owls have no such intentions. Someplace nearby the male owl has found a few suitable nests ready for occupancy. A desirable nest would be one built last year by a red-tailed hawk. There seems to be no hawk nest in the neighborhood, so the great horned owl may have his eyes on a crow's nest from last year. In any event, the great horned owls will not build a nest. They occupy nests built by other large birds. If the original owners return, the owls have nothing to fear. Instead, they inspire fear. Anyone who questions that has not looked closely at the talons of a great horned owl.

The intruding wild owl has a song that goes "hoo, hoo, hoo-raw!" At least, his song sounded like that until I read E. H. Forbush's translation of that last pair of syllables in his *Birds of Massachusetts*. Forbush heard them as "wu waugh." Forbush's ears probably were superior.

The owl concert starts almost the moment the sun drops below the horizon. The sky retains a dull brightness for a few moments and one can watch the bobbing and necktwisting of the wild soloist without artificial light. If one keeps walking slowly, the owl will permit one to pass within fifty feet of its perch. It tolerates loiterers but briefly. When it flies, the wingspread is about four feet.

Where does a bird two feet tall disappear to when dawn breaks? Like all large birds, or mammals for that matter, the great horned owl is not obvious in daylight. The soloist retires to a stand of red and white pines about a quarter-mile from the singing perch. I never have seen him there, but the crows and blue jays dash out of the pines with news that he is present.

What always has puzzled me is how crows and jays approach a great horned owl and live to scream about it. The owl can see better in daylight than I can. A great horned owl at a hawk-watch stand points out migrating hawks minutes before humans can find them.

The house in Trenton was southern in architecture. It dated to the War Between the States, maybe 1865. It was not elaborate. It had five rooms and each room had at least one door that led directly outdoors. The parlor had two doors that opened to the fresh air. A porch and porch roof entirely encircled the house. Thus one could step out onto the porch from any room and in any weather. Every door had a set of shutters and every window had shutters. The shutters had wooden panels in them that could be adjusted like venetian blinds. Also, the shutters were like Dutch doors, in that there were independent upper and lower halves. One could close the bottom shutters and leave the tops open. It was a valuable arrangement for hot summer nights. Missouri had many hot summer nights in that era long before air conditioning. The two outside doors, cut through opposite walls of the parlor, made social events possible in the room during summer. My father destroyed all these advantages as he modernized this house which had no central heat. It was the first house in which we lived that had electricity. It had a drop cord hanging down from the center of each ceiling. There was a bulb in the socket. If you were tall you might bump your head on it.

One day soon after we moved into the house I was experimenting with the shutters. Against the house on the inside of a bedroom shutter, I discovered a brown furry ball. A bit of probing disclosed that the ball was a female bat that wore a baby clutched to her front side. She threatened me with tiny teeth glistening from a tiny mouth. I was not impressed by her promised viciousness. I closed the shutter and let her be. It may have been my beginning as a naturalist.

Mar.

Fastest Gun in the East

The fastest gun in the East—the striped skunk—saunters New England byways in March after a winter's rest.

His presence becomes most noticeable in the morning when one may count along the highway the number of skunks that lost showdowns to automobiles the previous night. The toll seems to be highest in early spring when gentlemen skunks become traveling men. On these nights, a male skunk may shuffle along five miles, an unusual trek for an animal that otherwise rarely ventures more than a quarter to a half-mile from the home den.

The striped skunk is a two-gun character. He, or she, can fire ahead, behind, or to either side. Most prefer to bend their bodies into a U shape, so that they can score with maximum effectiveness and watch the result at the same time. Its main requirement is that it display its tail as an upright flag. Its artillery delivers maximum effect at five to ten feet—but the airborne drift at twenty feet is something that will linger long in memory, and in fact.

Possibly our most confident animal, the skunk remains unwilling to believe that his ammunition will not penetrate an automobile engine block. Thus he suffers many fatal accidents in our age. I say "accidents" because I doubt that any motorist would be foolish enough to run down a skunk. Certainly, anyone who purposely runs down a second skunk is in need of psychiatric help. At the time, his car must still smell some from the first one.

I have, in fact, had several hair-raising rides with drivers who swerved more than caution would allow in order to avoid a skunk. And none of these drivers was a sentimentalist.

The skunk's ammunition is quite different from the description generally given in folklore. It is a special secretion used for nothing except defense. Two glands located beneath the tail prepare the concoction. Each has a nipple which the skunk can aim voluntarily. When the skunk pulls the trigger, special muscles squeeze the glands, squirting the fluid.

If a skunk should miss on the first shot, it has nothing to worry about. It can fire five or six times.

The ingredient in skunk musk that leaves enemies gasping for breath and temporarily blinded is butyl mercaptan, an organic sulphur dioxide in a highly volatile oil base.

There is no ideal way to dissipate the chemical. If one encounters a skunk that puts up its flag and starts doing a little stamping jig, it is best to remember that. If your dog forgets, you can restore him to the family circle by rubbing a few dollars worth of canned tomatoes into his fur. For quite a while, the dog still will smell skunky any time it becomes wet. If your own clothing needs attention, a washing in excessive amounts of detergents probably comes as near sufficing as anything.

Fortunately, skunks are most reluctant to fire in anger. They give warnings and do everything they can—short of retreat—to avoid it. Many skunks live a lifetime without firing. It's a good thing too, since skunks live in number in the average suburban neighborhood. They seldom are seen, since they roam largely at night. Fortunately, they do not feel compelled to prove at random that they are top gun.

Spring Night Twitter

The twittering music over wet thickets in New England in March comes from a bird that sings with its wings.

The melody flows from the sky dance of the woodcock. The recital begins at dusk and the stage may be very close to your home. For woodcock will establish a singing ground even in closely built suburbs, if they can find a wetland thicket with an adjoining undisturbed meadow.

Unfortunately, an almanac listing of the hour and minute of sunset cannot serve as a reliable timetable for the wood-cock's performance. For the male woodcock times his de-but not by the clock but by the amount of daylight remain-ing. A photo meter can be a dependable guide. The wood-cock takes wing the moment sunlight diminishes to two foot-candles.

The "song" the woodcock beats out with his wings is among the remarkable sounds of nature. If, on hearing it, you doubt that such music originates from feathers, you are in good company. For centuries men argued about the source of a melody worthy of an excellent throat. But the music is mechanical. It comes from air vibrating through the three outer feathers on each wingtip.

Since light, rather than time, triggers the woodcock, the sky dance may occur at any hour on a moonlit night. Under these conditions the performance can be seen as well as heard. The bird rockets in steep ascent for about 200 feet and then spirals another 100 feet higher.

The twittering song occurs during the upward flight. After reaching a peak, the woodcock folds its wings and drops toward earth, occasionally interrupting the descent by unfolding the wings and swooping. As it drops, it begins a liquid "cheeping," generally known as the kissing song. The kissing song comes from the throat.

On return to earth, the bobwhite-sized woodcock struts like a miniature turkey and utters a "peenting" song, a buzzy "peent" quite similar to the call of the nighthawk. Since the woodcock has but the stubbiest of tails, when he spreads it like a turkey gobbler, he becomes a bit ridiculuous. His huge head and long bill make him appear off balance. He jerks his body from side to side as he "peents." His head bobs with each call. He gives the general impression of doing a little waltz.

One can watch the male woodcock perform on the ground from less than twenty feet. Indeed, in April when the fever of family life runs high, the male will strut and "peent" even when an observer turns a searchlight upon him.

The male woodcock spends about one minute in the air on each courtship flight. The evening's performance usually ends within an hour—although a bright moon may extend the engagement through the night. If one misses the evening recital, there is another each morning just before dawn.

The woodcock flight is among those things that must be seen to be appreciated. It tends, however, to develop an obsession that will have one out on cold dusks in early March looking for the first flier in the area. If you want to risk exposure to the experience, you probably can find a flying woodcock near some wetland or bog in your town—provided you do not live on Cape Cod, which is poor woodcock territory.

Undue pressure when applying a slate pencil to a slate causes an unpleasant squeak.

In fact, a slate rubbed with proper expertness can recreate the yelp of a wild turkey.

The yelp of the wild turkey today is even more common than the squeak of the slate. But it was not always thus.

When I reported for school in the first grade—there was no kindergarten in the village—I had a slate and slate pencil under my arm. The slate was a piece of natural slate framed by wood, with an extra cloth binder around the outside edges. The black surface was about eight-by-ten inches. It was used in American schools at one period as a savings on paper. The cost of paper, that was, not the trees that go into it and the like. A student wrote on the slate. After the teacher had inspected the math problem or English sentence, the student wiped the slate clean with a damp cloth.

The thing that was unusual about my slate was the fact that slates were out of style. My relatives all had used slates and they supposed that I should. Which only proved that like the remainder of humankind, they were at least twenty years behind the times.

Lucky 13

The opossum starts life in a raffle with fourteen as the unlucky number.

It may have entered the world with as many as forty-nine brothers and sisters, but the deck has been stacked against more than thirteen of them living.

This is because the opossum is "one of a kind" among North American mammals. The species is our only marsupial, a mammal which carries its undeveloped young in an abdominal pouch. The pouch contains but thirteen faucets. Each young opossum that reaches the pouch seizes a nipple and hangs on it for sixty days. Numbers fourteen and up are out of luck. Usually no more than eight succeed in finding the pouch, however. It is a minor miracle that any do.

At the time of birth—one might say, their first birth—opossums have developed no more than thirteen days. While

adult opossums are the size of small poodles, the young at this stage are the size of bees. They are blind little blobs of meat, with only the front paws developed. With the front paws, they climb through the mother's fur to the pouch where development into young opossums takes place.

While this may sound like intelligent action for what amounts to an embryo, it's about as smart as an opossum ever becomes. Opossums are most primitive mammals. Their brains are little more than knots to keep their spinal cords from unravelling, and the brain pan in the skull provides room for but a tiny knot. As they go through life, opossums seem to have little more judgment than caterpillars. They are among the few mammals that will walk along a rail until a train crushes them.

Yet, with almost everything in modern civilization seemingly against him, the opossum not only has thrived but has also moved into new territory. Before 1917 the opossum range was west of New York and southward from Illinois. Since then they have spread into New England and Ontario.

Opossums ocassionally are taken to the Massachusetts Audubon Society's Pleasant Valley Sanctuary in Lenox, proving that they exist wild in the rather inhospitable Berkshires. Last autumn two young opossums were delivered to the Stony Brook Nature Center in Norfolk by persons who had found them. But the incident that brought opossums to mind was my finding one that had been crushed by an automobile beside Route 140 in Franklin in late February.

The opossum—which becomes plain possum where the species is bountiful—is a southern mammal that reaches peak abundance below the Mason-Dixon Line. Although a furry mammal, it is poorly suited to life in our latitudes. Its ears and tail are rather bare and commonly become severely frostbitten in our colder winters.

As marsupials, opossums apparently are ancient animals, the last survivors in North America of an experimental model that Nature tried before shaping our modern placental mammals. With the exception of the opossum, the other marsupials failed to survive in a world where the more efficient modern mammals became predominant. Australia was the last great refuge of marsupials, with dozens of species surviving to the age of European settlement.

When opossums are touched, they go into a state of shock similar to death. It is from this state that the expression "playing possum" is derived. But before they are touched, many opossums put on a deceptive show of defensive ferocity. They snap their mouths and bare their teeth. When an opossum bares its teeth, it is a sight to behold. For opossums have fifty teeth, more than any other North American mammal.

Beat It, Kid

I once knew a wolf hunter. He was a taciturn type. I recognized him as an old man. He may have been twenty-five, considering my age at the time. His outfit drew my constant admiration. He had an old Durant which probably had been a touring car before he removed the body. He traveled with nothing except the engine and the chassis suspended by four, giant, wooden-spoked wheels. To drive he sat on the gasoline tank. The tank had been under the driver's seat, a location preferred by designers of that era, perhaps with the thought that, if the tank blew, the momentum propelling one toward kingdom come would not be lost.

The wolf hunter had a .30–.30 rifle and a bundle of traps too heavy for a farm boy to lift. Also tied on near the rear of the chassis was a saddle, and a canvas tarp bundled around his bedding, and perhaps a food supply. I frequently confronted the wolf hunter with conversation. So far as I can remember, his total contribution was a laconic, "Beat it, kid!"

I was pretty much of an aimless drifter even then. Occasionally I came upon the wolf hunter not too far from the village. Usually, under such circumstances, his tarp was bisected by a rope strung between two trees, which made it sort of a tent. He would be fishing in the creek.

Although my admiration of the wolf hunter was limited to his lifestyle, other members of the community were more impressed by his effectiveness. About every three months, the wolf hunter would putt into town with a wolf carcass slung over the gasoline tank. The trophy was taken to the county seat daily newspaper, where it was hung in the window for all to admire. Perhaps there was a bucket under the brute's mouth to collect any blood drip. I don't remember. But the window was rather well-equipped, since it was a favorite showplace for black squirrels, two-headed calves, four-legged chickens, and other cultural attractions.

Although the wolf hunter and I were biding our days in

the Missouri River drainage, where he got his wolves has become even more of a mystery to me now than it was then. I wore out lots of shoes, seldom left the village on the same compass direction twice, and could travel almost as fast and a lot more independently of roads than the Durant. And while I saw lots of other animals, I never saw any wolves. Coyotes occasionally, but not wolves. And the wolf hunter was getting wolves, not coyotes. Big gray wolves that must have weighed a hundred pounds.

Investigation later in life indicated that wolves had been extirpated in that county fifty years before I was born. But the wolf hunter was getting what he was paid to get, wolves.

It later was to occur to me, although it seemed never to occur to fellow townsmen, that perhaps when the wolf hunter picked up supplies at some remote railroad siding, he occasionally may have received a dripping crate in which some fellow wolf hunter had forwarded from farther west a well-iced wolf.

An intellectual vacuum in our age has been caused by the loss of the circus parade.

People today have television sets, stereo systems, and magnificent colored plates in books. One can buy tape decks filled with wisdom or criticism and play them in concert with a slide projector, creating a cultural atmosphere unattainable in years gone by. Expansion of cable television promises even more in entertainment and/or education.

The preceding agents of enlightenment were not available when I stood at the curb and watched circus parades. None fills the cultural gap left by the disappearance of the circus parade.

One never will be awed again by anything after having watched the Two-Hemispheres Band Wagon rumble by. This gilt-and-silvered resplendent vehicle weighed tons. The whole world was depicted on its sides. The circus band rode on top of the wagon, perhaps twelve feet above the street. And the vehicle was pulled by a sixteen-horse hitch.

March

At least, I remember it as sixteen horses. It could have been more or fewer horses. Childhood memories, after all, are fickle. But not so fickle that one cannot remember the wagons in a circus parade as the art equivalent to the Sistine Chapel.

How those wagons rumbled as the huge hubs turned on the axles and the wheels bounced along on the brick pavement!

Apr.

Little Mud-Smearer

Neighbors are at least as interesting as birds—and far easier to understand.

So it was easy to understand that he had a problem when my neighbor complained, "There's a little brown sparrow that keeps smearing mud on the shutter beside my front door."

It was early April. The season made it easy to identify the "little brown sparrow." Phoebes are in New England by that date and smearing mud on a shutter is typical phoebe behavior. The sparrow-sized flycatchers build their nests of mud and moss, like busy little plasterers. More often they choose a spot beneath a bridge or a barn cellar, and a few may even resort to the old-fashioned phoebe home site, a sheltered niche on a rocky cliff face.

But barns and suitable bridges have become premium sites today, so a few phoebes become domestic and try leasing a spot on the manor house.

My neighbor had attempted, by repeatedly wiping away the mud, to undomesticate the industrious pair that had encroached upon his shutter. But they were as persistent as he was. We held a brief consultation in which it was pointed out that phoebes are relentless pursuers of flying insects and might be of value near a front door. Since he was losing the battle anyway, the neighbor decided to permit the phoebes to complete their project.

For the next two weeks the phoebes devoted much of their energy to flying over my house—where a phoebe nest would be more welcome—and picking up bills full of mud from a bog, flying back over my house and plastering the

neighbor's shutter. Then the female phoebe laid four eggs in the nest.

Up to this point the actions of both the neighbors and the phoebes seemed to make sense, within certain limitations. Then, the phoebes broke the pattern. The nest and eggs were abandoned. The birds remained in the neighborhood and apparently built a nest at some other location. To get back to the beginning of this tale: the consternation of my neighbor who found himself in sole possession of a complete phoebe nest and a small mess of eggs was somewhat easier to understand than the phoebes' action.

When one mentions phoebes and associates them with spring (and they are most excellent harbingers of that season), he usually receives a few letters claiming that a flock of phoebes has inhabited a certain neighborhood "all winter."

The winter "phoebe" at these latitudes almost always proves to be the chickadee. While winter still holds a frosty grip on New England, the chickadee begins tuning a two-note whistle that sounds like "fee-bee." On days when a bright winter sun makes the snow blanket sparkle like diamonds, the "fee-bee" of the chickadee has a cheery spring promise—but a very premature one.

The certified song of spring is the phoebe's buzzy, low-toned conversation in which it repeatedly states its name in a monotone.

Too Much Credit to Kentucky

When man comes face to face with the trappings he carries around the world with him, he often fails to recognize a fellow traveler.

Take Kentucky bluegrass as an example. "Kentucky," indeed! This grass, now greening from Canada to the Carolinas, flourished in Rhode Island for decades before the English colonists corrupted the word "Caintuck" into "Kentucky." It probably grew in Massachusetts—and possibly even Connecticut, New Hampshire, and Maine—even before it reached Rhode Island.

The Roman legions grazed their horses on what we now know as Kentucky bluegrass. Maybe the cavalry of Attila the Hun was fueled by its green blades. For the same bluegrass was known to grow in Greece long before the Christian era, and possibly spread there from other sections of Europe or from Asia.

Even the generic name, *Poa*, belies the bluegrass origin. When the latter-day Adam, Linnaeus, gave a scientific name to Kentucky bluegrass, he called it *Poa*, referring to the early Greek name applied to forage grass.

Kentucky bluegrass is the meadow grass, or June grass, of British culture. Although bluegrass must have invaded the colonies much earlier, probably from seeds scattered by hay which was a common packing material or from hay brought for cattle, the earliest mention of it as "English grass" came in a report from Rhode Island in 1665.

Thomas Harriot in 1588 gave a "Brief and True Report of Virginia"—which probably was more brief than true. In it he mentioned lush grass. Possibly he meant salt marsh grass. Although the buffalo grass of the American West was one of the world's great forage grasses, there were no quality grasses along the Atlantic coast, except the grasses of the marshes.

The native forage grasses of New England were wild rye and broomstraw. Horses and cattle could live on these grasses in summer, but hay made from them was almost without value. They were mainly bulk, almost without nutrition. The poor quality of land grasses caused the colonists to turn to the salt marshes for cordgrass, reeds, and sedges to use as winter hay. The salt marshes became the "home meadows."

In colonial days, Kentucky bluegrass was known as Rhode Island grass—and also by its English names of June grass and meadow grass. Thus, it might have carried a New England name into our century—except for the remarkable quality of the limestone soils of Kentucky. When meadow grass reached the Bluegrass State, it became an almost unrecognized commodity. It grew thicker and more vigorously than it had grown on the sparse, acid soil of so much of New England.

Shortly before the Civil War, bluegrass began traveling under the name "Kentucky bluegrass." Oddly, Kentucky seems less than ideal for bluegrass. The state forms almost the southern perimeter of the grass's natural range, since bluegrass tends to die out in Tennessee. Bluegrass actually prefers a colder region, like New England—provided it can find the proper soil in which to sink its roots.

I attended my first circus when I was six weeks old.
I did not plan it. It just worked out that way. I was born in summer, which was the season of circuses. My father

had vowed that I should see every circus that ever visited our town. The first one came in six weeks.

It was, of course, because as a child he never got to go to the circus, that made my father so determined that I become a fan. Unlike so many adult vows, that one was kept. Much to my mother's distress, since she had to take me, my father bought reserved seats to every circus. Since we lived on the mainline of the Rock Island Railroad about halfway between Des Moines and Kansas City, some summers at least three circuses would play our town. All the circuses moved by rail. We saw all the great circuses—Barnum & Bailey, Sells–Floto, Ringling Brothers, Hagenbeck & Wallace—and all the little ones, too.

Most kids in the town from the day they saw the first circus poster pasted on a barnside spent their time hoping that their dad would be on the train crew that brought the circus to town. The circus always gave passes for everyone in the train crews' families. After Ringling Brothers and Barnum & Bailey combined, the circus moved on eight trains. It became a bonanza for railroad families.

And there were kids who watered the elephants, pumping the water and carrying it in buckets to those seemingly hollow animals. It was another route to tickets.

But underwritten by my father, I could watch the activities of others with the smug feeling that I had it made.

When You Know You're Right

The woman who helps me through the series of abrasions known as life looks out at the bird feeder each morning and invariably asks, "Are those birds pigeons or mourning doves?"

"Pigeons," I always answer, while continuing the ritual of drinking coffee.

Unfortunately, the other morning I actually looked through the window and the birds were mourning doves. I don't know how long the pigeons have been mourning doves. The situation could have existed all winter, for a few

mourning doves always remain in New England through the winter. Even as far north as Maine, especially along the coast.

The misidentification is not too embarrassing, however. At least ninety-five times out of one hundred, the dove-like birds at any feeder will be pigeons. Thus, ninety-five percent remains far higher than my average for accuracy.

A person who pondered these essays asked why I neglect the mourning doves. There are a few visiting her lawn, she said, and she wants to know more about them. I suppose the neglect can be summed up by the late Arthur C. Bent's comments in his *Life Histories of Birds*. He described it as common to abundant in New England in summer but generally overlooked despite its relatively large size because its dull plumage melts into the landscape.

Undoubtedly mourning doves are more frequently heard than seen. Bent wrote, "Just as the mockingbird in the southern states bursts suddenly into song and separates winter from spring, so the male mourning dove, who has been silent through the winter, at the first hint of spring begins to coo."

The "coo" of the mourning dove—to my tone-deaf ears—sounds a little like the dulcet tone of a mellow whistle on a faraway steam locomotive. So much so, that it is difficult for me to realize that eighty percent of the persons now alive never have heard a steam whistle, and therefore the description can mean nothing to them.

The main cohorts of mourning doves arrive in New England in late March and by the first week of April may have begun nesting. The nest usually is built in a coniferous tree, on a horizontal branch near the tree trunk. Usually there are two eggs, although there may be as many as four. The birds frequently breed twice in a summer.

But, perhaps we should get back to the earlier discussion. How does one determine whether the bird on the lawn is a pigeon or dove? First, let me make it clear that pigeons are doves. In the eastern Mediterranean where pigeons are native birds, they are called rock doves. In New England, a pigeon may be almost any color—although few have hues that would suggest a mourning dove. The mourning dove, on the other hand, comes in only one predominant plumage. In general, it is a tan-colored, slender pigeon which in flight displays a long, spade-shaped tail with white borders. Superimposed upon the tannish or brownish background are many iridescent colors. The trademark of the mourning dove is, as E. H. Forbush put it, "a small spot of black, glossed, blue, on side of head and upper neck beneath ear region." That's at least the approximate location of the spot.

Loneliness

What is the pinnacle of loneliness?

In nature, one might think of the spider who eats her mate seconds after meeting him as one destined to loneliness. But she later develops a maternal tenderness that keeps her social for the brief period in which the young abound. Or,

April

possibly one might select the chipmunk as loneliness exemplified, since except for the few days each year in which one half the population looks with favor upon the other half, chipmunks cannot tolerate company.

But the epitome of true loneliness occurs in a more familiar creature—the human. The observation reminds me of a letter which I received several years ago from an elderly woman who lived alone in an apartment. Part of the beauty of the letter lies in the fact that she never identified herself as lonely, at least, not in direct terms.

She wrote that her neighbors hated her, and that a few had referred to her in her presence as crazy. It apparently had troubled her less than one might suppose. But something had happened to her more recently that worried her. She had discovered a cricket in her kitchen and found it a rather joyful insect that often sang.

She had found the small black insect pleasant company, and this troubled her because she had been conditioned to dispatch insects found in the kitchen. What she wanted to know was, would I consider her odd if she asked advice on what to feed the cricket? She wondered if her attitude toward the cricket indicated aberrant behavior.

April

Fortunately, I could tell her truthfully that crickets long have been favored pets in the Orient. In fact, cricket cages in that region evolved into an art form as the wealthier had exquisite little jars carved for favorite crickets.

I suggested that the cricket probably was doing all right on its own in the kitchen, since it was alive and chirpy. But if she felt compulsion to feed the little critter, she might try offering a wet paste made from flour, or some tidbit such as a slice of apple. Actually, I'm not too certain about the nutritional demands of crickets but assumed that the suggested diet would be only supplementary at the most.

I also advised that a long-lasting relationship with crickets was unlikely if she did not consciously restrain herself from inadvertent use of pesticides in the house.

What interested me about the letter was a rather clear implication that a mind that had wandered to the ultimate fringes of loneliness seemed to have returned toward its natural center in response to a companion, in this case, a cricket.

How often must the insignificant influence our lives, for better or worse?

I did a two-year stretch in the Boy Scouts.

My mother made me do it. She made me become an Eagle Scout, too. At the ceremony awarding me the badge, the scout executive invited my mother to come up on the platform and pin the badge on me. She said that he did it because he knew that she was the one who actually had earned the award. Probably he did not know it, but I suppose she was correct.

I told my mother that if I had to, I might as well join the Boy Scout troop headed by the Presbyterian preacher. He recently had married and I reckoned he needed the money. Mother said no money was involved. I would, she said, join the American Legion's scout troop. There real men would teach me how to drill properly and make a man out of me. I joined the American Legion troop. It is a shame those real men failed.

April

I think the most important thing I learned in the Boy Scouts is that adults take volunteer jobs that they do not want. This I learned from an array of merit badge examiners. In the Boy Scouts one earns merit badges for passing tests. Like building a birdhouse, identifying fifty local birds, and thinking up at least one thing that birds might be good for—besides eating, that is—might get you a bird study merit badge. But one soon learned that study was unnecessary, except in rare instances. If one took a merit badge application form to the local examiner, the chances are that he would sign it to get rid of the precocious lad who stood before him. He took the job as examiner only because he was a merchant, salesman, lawyer, or physician and felt he should conform to a local image. Occasionally, someone who did not understand the system would ask the scout the required questions. In that case one might fail but could return in a week and pass the exam on the basis of information learned in the first unsuccessful encounter.

So the Boy Scouts taught better lessons in life than many adults realized.

May

The Loping Screamer

The unearthly wail attributed to the mythical banshees must have been patterned after the male red fox's weird scream.

The male fox that serenades my neighborhood indulges in this mad sound. Sometimes he does it early in the night. Sometimes at sunup. Why he ever does it is something that naturalists cannot answer. The call may occur in the autumn as well as spring. In any event he is not courting, for foxes have pups in the den in May—pups that soon will be coming out to play much like dog puppies.

When the neighborhood fox sounds off with his wild scream, he usually runs along a path that would be described as an arc of a circle. The ghastly scream occurs intermittently. A listener can almost plot the semicircle that the fox traveled by noting the points in wood and field from which the call came.

Surprisingly few naturalists have commented upon this weird cry which Ernest Thompson Seton referred to as the fox's "wild night cry." As good a description as any is that the scream sounds like a live animal being torn apart.

One of two naturalists whose remarks Seton cited was the Rev. John Bachman, an early American naturalist and friend of J. J. Audubon. Mr. Bachman reported that his neighbors in pursuit of the "peculiar and startling cries" supposed that they came from a mountain lion. They discovered, however, that they "proceeded from a red fox which was killed in the hunt got up for the purpose of killing the cougar."

The other naturalist cited by Seton, Samuel Scoville, Jr., while equally unable to describe the indescribable scream,

gave a better idea of the human reaction to the night cry. Reporting on his observations one October night in the New Jersey Barrens, Scoville said:

"Suddenly the stillness was broken by a perfectly appalling scream. Although I recognized what it was, my muscles jerked and twitched at the sound, and when it was repeated, my companion, even though a veteran naturalist, gripped me so tightly that his fingerprints showed black on my arm the next morning.

"It was the scream of a fox, probably the most sinister, unearthly, wild animal note that can be heard in North America. The howl of the wolf and the screech of the wildcat, or bay lynx, are all weird sounds, to say nothing of the frightful shriek which the horned owl sometimes gives, but none of them begins to be as fearful as the scream of the dog (male) fox."

May

Your dog most likely will agree with Scoville's description of the fearful aspects of the fox's cry. For, when the male fox gives a concert, the barking dogs of a neighborhood are strangely silent.

It's not what the eye sees but what the brain records that counts.

One learned such facts early when the century was young.

My father bought me a single-shot .22-calibre rifle when I was eight years old and took me hunting. We were moving through a mild snowstorm, searching for cottontail rabbits. I had seen rabbits, had raised them, in fact. And like most children had seen rabbit pictures in books. But as father advised, one looks not for rabbits but for black shiny buttons when hunting in a snowstorm. The cottontails would hunker down next to a tree trunk and take advantage of the snow-and-wind physics that create a shallow bowl around the base of a tree. The snow spangled rabbit blends into the landscape. Therefore, the only obvious telltale object that one can seek is the rabbit's open eye.

That's why I was not surprised when Ludlow Griscom pointed out the first bald eagle I ever had seen. It stood on the snow-covered ice of the Merrimack River. Its white head and tail disappeared into the snow background. All that remained visible were the black wings which created a form that looked like a coal bucket. It was an old-time coal bucket that modern readers might not recognize. But that is what one searching for bald eagles against the snow should look for.

If seeing is believing, one faces many disappointments. At least, the experiences of my sometimes cynical life advise against any such acceptance of anything.

Gathering Bracken Seed

The distance that separates modern man from his natural environment may be indicated by the fact that bracken no longer mystifies him.

Or, to put it into more comprehensible terms that most modern men lack any conception of what bracken may be, and have never heard of the mass of folklore that once surrounded this rather common wild fern.

Bracken bore the imprint of the devil. Its seeds could be gathered only by witches. Bracken seed held miraculous cure for anything that ailed man, including poverty. Indeed, under proper moon phases in spring, sheets were spread beneath bracken plants to capture seeds, since possession of bracken seed assured one of immediate wealth.

May

In an age when most men lived a rural existence, almost all citizens knew these "facts" about bracken.

Although our conscious familiarity with the devil's imprint seems too limited for judgment, the other bits of folklore surrounding bracken unquestionably are true! They are true because bracken, in common with other ferns, has no seeds!

Bracken in May is uncoiling its fronds. It probably is the commonest fern in Massachusetts.

In an era in which superstition and botany were more closely allied than they are today, scientists looked for "signatures" in plants. If they found it had seeds that looked like human teeth, something about the plant must be good for the toothache, etc. Bracken had but one thing favorable in signatures; its palmate frond (leaf) bore three different styles of leaflets. The lower parts of the frond are doubly pinnate (indented), the next higher section is singly pinnate, and the tips of the blades are undivided. Three and seven rank high in Western numerology and should have given the bracken considerable status.

But bracken refused to produce seed—as a plant supposedly should. It did, however, spread as though it were shedding seeds. This was suspicious. By cutting cross sections, the herbalists discovered that the stem was formed exactly as the footprint of the devil! They were quite familiar with the devil's footprints in those days.

Thus, the evidence was clear. The method through which bracken and other ferns spread involved witchcraft. The seeds were there, but they were enchanted and invisible. Perhaps a witch could see them. But not ordinary mortals.

Today we know that ferns are primitive plants, indeed, that they reigned among the earth's vegetation in that early dawn before plant seeds evolved. They spread by spores, a dust so fine that only a good microscope makes the details of a grain visible. Ferns lead two lives. A grain of spore that lands in a favorable location grows into a prothallus, a pinhead bit of green protoplasm that looks like a minute liverwort. In due time, the prothallus combines its male and female cells and, as it dies, a fern is born.

The only part of modern ferns that appears above ground

in our latitudes are the leaves. Thoreau, observing this, commented, "Nature made ferns for pure leaves to see what she could do in that line."

Poets' Bird

A gang of holdovers from horse-and-buggy days passed through a nearby field recently.

They were bobolinks, more than one hundred of them, all males. It was a sight seldom seen today. An earlier generation of New Englanders might have wondered about my haste to reach the field and see these now uncommon migrants. For bobolinks were common birds of the region, at least into post–Civil War days.

Indeed, in years when my summers were heated by hot winds off the Great Plains, I supposed that were I ever to reach New England, the rare bobolink along the Missouri River would become a commonplace bird. The New England poets treated them so. Alas, the poets' era was a much earlier one.

Our first acquaintance with the bobolink arose from a small card found in a box of baking soda. It depicted a most unusual bird. It was a blackbird with a white back and buffy feathers at the nape of the neck.

In that unliberated age the baking soda manufacturer had the nerve to show only the male bird. But the male is the interesting bobolink. The females wear subdued dingy browns, as befits a bird that nests on the ground. Only the male sports a white back and black undersides, the reversal of normal color distribution in birds.

Bobolinks perhaps reached their zenith of population when horsepower came wrapped in horsehide. Hayfields then flourished near urban centers, supplying hay and bedding for city horses. The bobolink nests in tall grass. By the turn of the century, bobolinks were on the downgrade in New England. Early conservationists were designing flush bars which would precede the cutter bar of horse-drawn hay cutting machines. It was supposed that the cutter bars were destroying young bobolinks inexperienced with mechanical hay cutting. An earlier generation had cut hay by scythe.

Actually, farms were on the wane and open land was disappearing into woods. At the same time, bobolinks were being shot by the thousands in the South as market game. Bobolinks brought gunners twenty-five cents per dozen cleaned birds. The birds were sold in northern markets at seventy-five cents to one dollar a dozen, and were considered fare for spendthrift epicures. It gives one a dimension of money value in those days.

Bobolinks still breed in New England and in the Maritimes, but in reduced numbers. A recent survey found the birds using the pastures of defunct or dying dairies. The fields had been abandoned a year or two and weeds were intruding upon the grass. Almost all sites were near ponds.

In most instances, the days of the birds' tenancy were numbered. The fields were to become housing sites. Even if they were not, trees soon would make the field unattractive to bobolinks.

The survey, oddly enough, was begun because New Englanders of today are not certain what sort of sites bobolinks prefer. Once they seemed to be everywhere. Now nothing seems to serve them.

Popping Like Ping-Pong Balls

The local mallard duck is back trying again.

Somewhere out there in the tall vegetation, not more than three hundred yards from the typewriter tapping out these words, the mallard sits on a clutch of eggs. Her internal rigging, of course, makes her do it. But what on earth keeps her spirits up? Or, more to the point, what makes her try around here again, considering her dismal record of continued failures?

Sometime around June first, the mallard's present secretiveness will end. She and I will encounter in a particular unmowed field of two-foot tall grass. She will suddenly rocket skyward from the grass, quack excitedly, and fly a short distance, ending the crippled flight with a plunge toward earth. I am supposed to chase her. Instead, I look for the flock of ducklings, which may be six or a dozen.

When I eventually come upon the ducklings' hiding place, the mallard hen will change the melody of her quacking. Apparently it is a signal that Plan A (hiding quietly) must be abandoned for Plan B (run for your lives). Plan B strikes the flock of little brown and buff fluffs about the way heat affects popcorn. They begin popping up and down like ping-pong balls dropped from a table. Each heads in a different direction, traveling like a person trying to ride a pogo stick through tall corn.

Since there still are mallards on this earth, the strategy must work somewhere. But in four springs it has not brought success to the mallard and her brood. The family tries it in an area well populated by dogs and cats, and likely a few rats. Within a week the mallard hen is alone.

The site fidelity of the mallard probably is not too rare among birds. As a friend pointed out recently, a female northern (formerly Baltimore) oriole landed in his yard, and before the day ended, she had begun constructing a nest. Her seeming familiarity suggested that she was back home for another summer.

Banding of mallards, in regions where they are valued birds, proves that the female returns to her preferred area and brings a drake along with her from the wintering grounds. The drake may vary, indeed, usually does. But her nesting area continues to be the same, so long as there is a pool of water within a half-mile or so of the nest site.

Mallards have a poor image among bird watchers in New England. And among ecologists, too. Many mallards got their start by escaping from farms—or, at least, their ancestors did. The native mallard-form duck is the black duck. Mallards supposedly are replacing the native duck. Perhaps what really is happening is that the mallards' adaptability to human intrusions enables the birds to breed in areas which black ducks, which are less tolerant, have abandoned.

The mallard offers a supreme test of prejudicial thinking. Look at a wood-duck drake and a mallard drake in spring plumage, and make a decision concerning comparable beauty. If the decision casts the wood duck as exquisite and the mallard as trash, then it is preconditioned. In its green chestnut, blue, black, and white, the mallard drake equals any and surpasses most ducks. Those who fail to see it that way are looking into their minds while peering through binoculars.

It was with the .22-calibre rifle that I learned why the U.S. government frowns upon we citizens killing its ducks with a rifle.

Probably it was against the law when I did it, but one

may be assured today that putting rifle slugs in ducks can cause a costly headache of the federal court type.

The land where I was born had been badly scarred. After World War I some scalawags came among the residents with an impressive ditching machine. They convinced the farmers that turning the Grand River (it really was the east fork of the Thompson River, but folks talked in grand terms) into a straight ditch would solve all their problems. Among other things there never would be another flood. In those days no one realized that the intermittently flooded river floodplain was rich because of flood-borne silt.

The ditching was to affect my hunting methods more than anything else that touched my life orb. I discovered that by lying flat on the rim of the deep canyon that ditching had created, one could shoot ducks at considerable distance. The ducks were below and either upstream or downstream from the shooter. The rifle made only a quiet "pop." The struck duck collapsed as though stricken by a heart attack. The duck's companions seemed interested but unalarmed by the victim's fate. One could shoot a flock of ducks unless something other than the shooter spooked them.

Perhaps it was not sporting. But I was collecting meat. If the whole thing had been for "sport" I would not have bothered.

June

Homing in on Humans

For a comparatively rare New England insect, the mosquito attracts considerable attention.

Sounds strange to call mosquitoes rare? Their habits rather than numbers make mosquitoes seem abundant. The grass, bushes, and trees carry loads of insects. But, of all the hordes, only the mosquito seeks you. There may be thousands of other insects that you seldom see, but if there are five female mosquitoes, they will home in on you like a surface-to-air rocket headed for a plane.

Perhaps you never thought of mosquitoes as being flies, distant relatives, in fact, of the house fly. Nor, that there are more than 2500 species of mosquitoes around the world, and that most species live on such food as nectar and never bite humans nor any other animal.

Mosquitoes have at least two clues that alert them to the presence of a human or other warm-blooded creature, body heat and carbon dioxide. Experiments indicate that female mosquitoes will be attracted to any source of heat that is ten degrees warmer than the prevailing climatic temperature. The human temperature of 98.6 degrees usually supplies such a differential with air temperatures, especially in the coolness of dawn or dusk when most mosquitoes fly.

The mosquitoes' sensitivity to carbon dioxide—which is a major component of any animal's breath—seems associated with appetite. Researchers who raise colonies of mosquitoes for experiments have discovered that the most efficient method of inducing them to feed is to breathe into the mosquito container. Mosquitoes which have shown no interest in food suddenly become very hungry in the presence of carbon dioxide.

A diet deficiency in youth causes adult female mosquitoes to seek blood. *Culex pipiens,* the common house mosquito, cannot develop eggs without a blood meal. Its near relative, *Culex molestus,* however, can produce eggs while living on a diet of nectar. The difference between them, investigators believe, consists of the amount of protein each species accumulated while in the larva (non-flying) stage.

Culex molestus has a heavy charge of protein in its body when it takes wing from its watery nursery. *Culex pipiens,* on the other hand, does not contain enough protein to form yolks for its eggs. Thus, it must obtain protein by sucking blood.

Male mosquitoes do not bite people. Their mouths are shaped quite differently from the females', making it impossible for them to bite. The males live on saps and nectar.

Temperature and humidity affect—almost to the point of control—the activities of mosquitoes. They prefer warm, rather than hot, temperatures and high humidity. These conditions occur at dusk and dawn, which is why most mosquitoes become active at these periods. Most mosquitoes will not fly in hot, dry sunshine. Their bodies are inefficient in controlling loss of moisture, and dry heat can kill them.

The control of mosquitoes has vexed men since prehistory. Most measures that have been tried—from the draining of Rome's Pontine Marshes to the use of DDT—have caused widespread damage to desirable wildlife.

Awakened by an Oriole

Each weekday morning I am awakened by the roar of automobiles.

Although the bedroom windows almost overhang a highway whose traffic flows to Boston, the fact that the roar awakens me really should be surprising. For I have slept

through the night about 100 feet from a stop sign that inter-
rupts the steady stream of gasoline tank trucks that supply
the western suburbs for a major oil company. Each of these
growling mammoths goes through at least six complaining
gear shifts before regaining the momentum that carries it
beyond ear range. Weary guests often comment on the
trucks at breakfast.

What led to this recital was a recent complaint from a
lady. She asked for advice on how to solve a most perplex-
ing problem. She is awakened each morning by the song of
an oriole. Needless to say, my heart goes out to her. Anyone who today can afford the luxury of living in such quiet
solitude perhaps could afford ear plugs. Not that I suppose
money can solve all problems. But it can give one a choice
of awakening devices.

I realize, unfortunately, that the oriole-flustered lady is
not alone in this world stuffed with anxiety. A favorite
in-law (if one has favorites in that category) was disturbed
by a few frogs that lived in a pool near her bedroom. Now if
there is anything more usable than frog or insect music in
giving a rest to those ghostly sheep that might otherwise
have to jump over an imaginary fence for counting, I don't
know what it is. Frog music must be the voice of Morpheus
personified. But this in-law was driven nuts by it. At least
she accounted for her obvious aberrant behavior by blaming
the frogs. To solve it, her son bought her a battery radio.
Each night she lay with the thing blatting away under her
pillow and slept as though sleep was a just reward.

I stoop to such obscenity only to illustrate that there is no
accounting for lack of taste. When rock-and-roll sounds
better than frogs, one has become a casualty of civilization.
When the song of an oriole lacks the reassurance that all is
well and one can sleep on, then one may have fallen victim
to the syndrome that accepts mechanized rhythm as natural.
These are serious flaws in the soul. They indicate that there
has been a malfunction recently in a couple million years of
human evolution that prepared mankind for birds or frogs.
There was no preparation for the whine of gears.

One who can awaken to the snap of a twig or the fall of a
rock has a full inheritance. He or she has the tribal memory

of saber-toothed tigers or unexpected avalanches. If one awakens to an oriole's cry of alarm, then all is well with the old subconscious. These have survival value. Treat them as rare wine. But, when one awakens to a signal that all is well—like the uninterrupted song of frogs or morning gladness of the oriole—well, one has tuned in on the wrong signals. He or she will find many things wrong in life, and because of the orientation, should not be surprised.

My best friend had an unusual 10-gauge double-barreled shotgun.

He had to carry it on his shoulder like a soldier when it was loaded. The reason was that as we walked rhythmically along the railroad right of way, stepping from tie to tie, the vibrations would release the firing pins in the hammerless gun. The gun sometimes went boom boom *as the barrels discharged in sequence. Other times it would go* blaamm, *both barrels firing simultaneously.*

My friend and I were about ten years old. We were modern gunners for the period. Our weapons, actually household hunting arms, used paper shells, the very latest ammunition. The kids and adults who used brass shells had us bested economically, but they had other problems. They loaded the brass shells with powder and shot at home and could reuse them many times. But the brass shells when fired often swelled so tightly in the chamber that the gunner had to punch them out with a long wire rod which was carried for such emergencies. A few still used muzzle-loading guns. Those gunners were not the Sunday afternoon dilettante muzzle-loader gunners of today. They were for real.

The guns we all had were made with Damascus twist steel. The process fabricated a dangerous gun, liable to rip open along the top of the barrel if the muzzle was blocked by mud or snow.

I doubt that any modern insurance company would have insured my life. But my mother always told everyone that she carefully supervised me.

Farewell to a Falcon

That peregrine falcon that I've been awaiting isn't coming back.

Unfortunately, the feds found him in a taxidermist's shop down in New Jersey. The last I saw him was at 6:35 P.M., August 26, 1975. At the time, he and another falcon, most probably a nest mate, were flying in a circle high above Lincoln, Massachusetts. Two months earlier, on June 23, 1975, those two falcons and another which later may have been electrocuted, were downy white chicks delivered to the Massachusetts Audubon Society at Lincoln for rearing and release in the wild. They were products of the Pere-

grine Project, one of those pet projects of mine with which I bore the more literate among readers.

Well, it seems that the Lincoln-reared peregrine made it to Cranbury, New Jersey, in time for the Labor Day weekend. It was during that period at Cranbury that a gentleman shooting pigeons noticed two peregrines present and naturally shot one of them. Whether the other peregrine was wounded I do not know.

Noting that he had a rather unusual prize, indeed, an endangered species, the gentleman gunner took it home and put it in deep freeze. Apparently, the gentleman's logic followed my own. I always felt that if I were to delay reporting my misdeeds of Monday until Thursday my old man would react less vigorously, the four-day cooling off period supposedly having mellowed him as well as me. Anyway, the gentleman let the peregrine literally cool several months until he decided it was safe to take it to a taxidermist. As it turned out, he was safe in getting it to the bird stuffer. Someone else blew the whistle.

The bird in New Jersey could be identified as a Lincoln-reared peregrine because the killer had left the Peregrine Project band on the bird's leg. Apparently he regarded it as certification that the bird was a peregrine.

While it is not difficult to be less joyful than Pollyanna over the discovery that a peregrine whom I knew personally now stares through glass eyes, the discovery does have a positive aspect. It proves that at least one—and I'm certain, two—Lincoln-reared peregrines not only were keeping themselves alive, but also, in traveling south along traditional peregrine routes, the birds were acting normally.

For some reason, the Lincoln peregrines always were treated as though they were retarded. Possibly it was because one of them disappeared early, supposedly electrocuted when he landed on a transformer and the radio aerial on his tail touched a power line. Actually, the bird never was found. His supposed demise was based upon the fact that he went off the air quite suddenly while a directional antenna was being used in tracing him.

The experiences of the Lincoln peregrines indicate that

the attempt to restore peregrines in the East, where they were wiped out by DDT, can succeed. All that is needed is the release of enough peregrines to overcome natural losses and an occasional marksman.

Also, the Peregrine Project can furnish the courts with an estimate of the price of a peregrine, since the project keeps cost accounts. It no longer is necessary for a judge to worry whether a five-dollar fine for shooting a peregrine is too much.

If I had had a better grasp of judgment, I would have been the spelling champion of Grundy County.

I still recall the scene. It was a sweaty, hot, May afternoon and we were gathered in the First Baptist Church in Trenton, the county seat. At least thirty-five of us 10-to-11-year-olds were locked in mortal intellectualism. Anyone who misspelled a word was out of the contest. And we were the cream of spellers in the rural county.

The afternoon ground on and finally the two left standing were myself and this prissy girl whose name has faded from memory. She had two long braids of hair and a too-good-to-be-true attitude.

The judge asked me to spell judgement. I spelled it just as I have written it in this paragraph. That twit of a girl spelled it as I spelled it in the first paragraph of this account. She became the champion speller of Grundy County.

I never again forgot two things: (1) how to spell judgment, and (2) how much I hated that now nameless but still too sweet girl. I was always a sore loser.

A Holdover Dragon

June is the season of dragons.

In southern New England, dragons are abroad mostly in June, but a bit into July.

June

What dragons? Gracious, aren't you familiar with the snapping turtle? If ever there was a holdover from that era when the Earth was a damp, dark, and shapeless void, it must be the snapping turtle. While it is true that we speak of crocodiles and alligators as "the last ruling reptiles"— implying that these elongated suitcase covers inherited the legacy of the dinosaurs—the expression overlooks the snapping turtles' success. Who knows of a crocodile that inhabits areas as diverse as Nova Scotia and Ecuador? The snapping turtle does.

The dragon quality of the snapping turtle becomes most apparent when one views the turtle from the side at rather close quarters. It is not a recommended position. If you try it, do it on your own. Get too close and you may be surprised at the speed of the snapping turtle, which can strike—well, it seems as fast as a rattler. However, from a side view, one can see the saw-toothed sail along the snapper's tail, a serrated bit of flesh that reminds one of the dragon which St. George killed. Remember?

One seldom sees snapping turtles at any time other than early summer. Snapping turtles spend their lives under water and are so secretive that they can survive in areas as urban as New York's Central Park. In June, however, the females leave the ponds and streams to lay eggs. Most snappers are satisfied to lay eggs within thirty to fifty feet from their aquatic home. But some travel a few hundred yards, and sometimes quite high up a hill.

Snapping turtle eggs remind one of table tennis balls, being white spheres about one inch in diameter. The female snapper excavates a flask-shaped hole with her hind legs and drops the eggs into it. One hears of seventy-five-egg snapper nests. But one seldom sees a nest with more than twenty-five eggs. While female snapping turtles mask the next site, most nests are dug up by skunks or raccoons. The nests that escape predation hatch in about ninety days, the sun providing the warmth for incubation. Young turtles have to evade a posse of land predators on the way to a pond and then must avoid being consumed by bass or pickerel until they acquire heft.

Almost anything associated with the snapping turtle tends to become superlative: the biggest, meanest, etc. So one hears about forty-to-fifty-pound snapping turtles. Occasionally one even sees a captive overfed snapping turtle whose obesity tips seventy pounds. However, in the wild a snapping turtle that passes twenty pounds is extraordinary. Some run thirty pounds.

Although supposedly a specialist in ducks and game fish, snapping turtles have an appetite for anything. As for destroying snappers because of their predation, I like best the comment of my biology mentor, Dr. James D. Lazell, Jr., "Such killing can only be justified by the belief that Europeans arrived here only just in time to save our waterfowl from extinction at the jaws of their native predators."

July

Missing the Mark on Moles

It is fortunate that nothing of value rests upon the average New Englander's ability to identify a mole.

For the truth is that when a New England nature buff reports that he or she has seen a mole, ninety-nine times out of a hundred he or she has seen a short-tailed shrew instead.

This particularly is true of the common report, "I saw a mole run across the road."

Moles can "swim" through the earth, doing a breast stroke with their spade-like front feet, but running across the road would be most difficult for them. The hairy-tailed mole, most common to New England uplands, would be the most likely mole candidate for running, since its front feet are less spade-like than other moles. The hairy-tailed even comes out of its tunnels on some nights and feeds on insects in the forest floor litter. But its broad front feet limit its skill at running.

So, the "mole" that runs across the road with the speed and agility of a mouse is the short-tailed shrew.

Perhaps shrews are mistaken for moles because they have plush fur, pointed muzzle, tiny eyes, and short tails, all characteristic of moles. Shrews also tunnel through the litter on a forest floor. In addition, shrews will travel the tunnels made by any other small animal. But shrews leave the deep ploughing of soil to their distant cousins, the moles.

Since New Englanders seem satisfied in thinking of shrews as moles, we will dismiss the moles with the statement that New England has three: the common mole, which is not "common" anywhere in New England and rarely occurs north of a line drawn through Worcester, Mas-

sachusetts; the star-nosed mole, which ranges into Canada, prefers wetlands and frequently swims; and the hairy-tailed mole, mentioned earlier, which ranges through northern New England but seldom occurs farther south than northern Connecticut and Rhode Island.

The short-tailed shrew, which is large for a shrew but roughly half the size of a mole, occurs throughout New England. On two of Massachusetts' outer islands, Martha's Vineyard and Nantucket, the short-tailed shrew populations have been isolated from the mainland long enough to evolve slightly different coloration and smaller size. The shrews on these islands are considered two distinct subspecies.

Persons who never have seen a short-tailed shrew may be surprised to learn that in "good" years there may be as many as 250 short-tailed shrews on a single acre. And this acre may be very close to your home.

Like moles, shrews feed principally upon insects. Shrews, however, are more aggressive than moles and feed also on other small mammals. They are known to kill mice, and some mammalogists consider shrews the most valuable little animal to man that lives in agricultural areas. The estimate is based upon an enormous harvest of both mice and insects by shrews, which daily consume an amount of food equivalent to their own weight. Their consumption of food can be compared to a 175-pound man eating 175 pounds of meat daily.

Shrews have been known to kill animals the size of small rabbits. Charles E. Roth, mammalogist with the Massachusetts Audubon Society, has found evidence of shrews attacking such large edible items as the carcass of a winter-killed deer. If all other food sources fail, shrews eat other shrews, for they burn fuel so fast that they starve quickly without a steady food supply.

The janitor of the Hodge Presbyterian Church was very black and his name was Pansy.

His name was not John William Pansy. Nor was it Pansy J. Williams. His name was Pansy, period.

Even as a small child I thought that strange.

It turned out, however, that Pansy had been born a slave. He was freed while in diapers. That, however, did not change the fact that he had been given just one name, like maybe one might name a dog. Apparently it never bothered Pansy. He did not pick up another name as other blacks did, nor did he drop the original.

I knew people who claimed to have seen a widow of a Revolutionary War veteran. I have seen the widow of a Mexican War veteran, which was not too unusual since most of the men who fought that war were from the Missouri and Mississippi River Valleys. I knew a couple of Confederate veterans and can remember when a dozen of them lived in the state Confederate home at Higginsville.

I even had the honor of serving as a page at one of the last state conventions of Union veterans in Missouri. It was in the old Trenton Hotel across the street from the courthouse. And I cannot believe that it happened so long ago.

Thoreau's Night Warbler

The wild, sweet song of Thoreau's "mysterious night warbler" awakened me at a recent midnight.

It was a loud, clear song quite unlike any heard in daylight. A southerner might have mistaken it for the nocturnal music of a mockingbird. Indeed, had it not been for Charlotte Smith of the Massachusetts Audubon Society, the night bird would have been as much a mystery to me as it was to Thoreau throughout his lifetime.

Thoreau almost solved the mystery once. But, he failed to follow through on his May 19, 1858, note in his journal, "Heard the night warbler begin his strain just like an oven-bird!"

The night warbler is the ovenbird. Mrs. Smith called my attention to the late Edward Howe Forbush's comments,

which include a colorful description of the song. He wrote, "One evening as I lingered in the woods until twilight came, I heard in the air a wild outburst of intricate rapturous melody ascending far above the treetops, and saw the little singer rising against the glow of the western sky, pouring out his passion song to the slowly rising moon."

The night singer of my neighborhood sings from the white pine stand near the house. He sings later than twilight, although to the best of my memory, he requires moonlight. The song seldom happens more than once a summer. The fact that the loud liquid notes awaken me speaks highly of the tone volume. Anyone aware of the volume of the ovenbird's "teacher, Teacher, TEACHER" song—which is among the more familiar woodland songs in New England— will appreciate the ovenbird's loudness.

Singing at night is unusual for a songbird. It is a time for owl calls or night heron squawks. The ovenbird, however, uses darkness to break the monotony of his familiar song pattern.

Forbush notes that: "Thoreau speaks often of this 'mysterious night warbler' but apparently never identified it. His anxiety to know the source of this night melody was so great that Emerson warned him to cease trying to find out what it was lest he succeed and 'thereafter lose all interest in life.'"

The late Dr. Frank M. Chapman said of the ovenbird's night song, "It is a wild outpouring of jumbled notes over which the bird seems to have no control, and is often concluded with the common 'teacher' song."

The ovenbird is a warbler whose life pattern is so thrush-like that it once was known popularly as the golden-crowned thrush. The birds live in mature forests. The male usually sings from a large branch less than halfway up a tree. The female devotes most of her time to scurrying about on the forest floor searching for insects. The ovenbird is named for its nest. Built on the forest floor, the nest usually has an arched roof over it with a side entrance, much like the old ovens that were in the sides of colonial fireplaces.

Henny Penny Remembered

There was a horrid little red hen with which teachers tortured boys in knickers who did not know how to read and showed scant promise of learning.

This miserable fowl was sometimes known as "Henny Penny" or other ridiculous, familiar names in hopes of making her exploits, which did not amount to much, more entrancing to the literarily recalcitrant. It was a period in which *McGuffey's Reader* recently had faded from the scene, and all my adult relatives were convinced that without McGuffey the world was drifting toward rot.

I wouldn't bother people with all this, except that I need to explain why Rhode Island's state bird does not thrill me. That bird is the Rhode Island Red, a chicken which my childish mind confused with the little red hen.

As state birds go (and not one of them goes very far), I suppose that the Rhode Island Red is as good as the next. It may equal Massachusetts' chickadee and New Hampshire's purple finch. The Rhode Island Red is a state native. And we suspect that it is an endangered "species." The computer has imperiled the future of all feathered thoroughbreds.

Even before the computer, chickens were beginning to lose status as bluebloods. When I was a child, farmers boasted about the purity of their Anconas, Black Minorcas, Rhode Island Reds, Barred Rocks, Partridge Wyandottes, etc. But about the time I began shaving, farmers were ordering unnamed but numbered chicken breeds, like X2425. These were what we would have considered mongrels. But poultry husbandry had progressed to the point where chicken gene pools were being manipulated to produce either rapidly maturing meat birds or sensational egg layers.

It is fortunate that the Red was produced in Rhode Island because it never could have become alliterative if it had originated in Massachusetts. But it barely escaped a Bay State beginning. The critter was put together in Adamsville,

Rhode Island, and one must be careful where one steps in Adamsville or one will accidentally step on Massachusetts. The line brushes the village and with a little practice one could stand in Westport, Massachusetts, and read the inscription on the monument erected to the Rhode Island Red in Adamsville. In fact, John Macomber of Westport was cooperating with Capt. William Tripp of Adamsville when they began crossbreeding chickens in 1854. Isaac C. Wilbur of Little Compton (Adamsville is a village of Little Compton) supposedly gave the new creation the name of Rhode Island Red, which wasn't too bad a choice, considering that the chicken was red. Somebody later developed a white Rhode Island Red, but that is a complicated color scheme that shall not be discussed here.

Tripp and Macomber went back to original stock in their search for the ultimate chicken. They obtained Malay and Java junglecocks and bred them with Cochin China hens. The junglecocks are original, undiluted, wild chicken stocks. The resulting chickens were then crossed with light Brahmas, Plymouth Rocks, and brown Leghorns. The final product, the Rhode Island Red, was recognized as a legitimate breed in 1895.

My father was undecided.

He liked both the Star and the Chevrolet. They were more or less identical touring cars. Black bodies, fold-down tops, windshields split horizontally like a venetian blind, and side curtains for rainy weather stowed under the back seat.

So far as most of us knew, the Star was as much a winner as the Chevrolet. There were many good cars: Veeley, Reo Flying Cloud, Durant, Hupmobile, Oakland, Studebaker, Stutz, Packard—a wide variety.

My grandmother said she wanted the Chevrolet. It was her money so her choice prevailed. Maybe her decision wiped out the Star. The manufacturers might have continued if they could have disposed of that one car.

The roads we drove over were dirt. The only pavement

was in the cities, usually brick, although poured concrete was under development. A sensible drive was the twelve-mile round trip to Tindall. An experience was the twenty-five-mile round trip to Farmersville. Most travel was only about twice as fast as a horse could accomplish. There were frequent stops for flat tires. The car wheels had wooden spokes. The rim was demountable and was split. The two features made it easier to change or repair a tire.

One day when the road to Farmersville had been freshly gravelled, my father decided to open up the engine in a straight stretch. The car's speedometer inched up to forty-five miles an hour. You should have heard my mother's screams of terror. There was a huge plume of dust behind us. It was pretty scary.

Yankee Character Defect

Some character defect among New Englanders keeps them killing milk snakes under the impression that they are rattlesnakes.

This is an aberrant behavior. In almost all other regions the citizens beat milk snakes into a pulp under the impression that they are copperheads. While such activity makes little sense, the outlanders at least show better judgment. The milk snake has no rattle and could not possibly be a rattlesnake. However, New Englanders have so few opportunities to kill snakes, things being as they are, that they should be forgiven for killing what they don't know. It is after all an expression of a phobia, such as my own illogical fear of heights.

Perhaps there is little to be gained in reporting that the milk snake does not milk cows. That old tale perennially has been laid to rest but rises from the ashes as though it were a Phoenix. It is part of a worldwide foolishness about snakes, different species of quite unrelated serpents having been assigned the dishonor. Locally, the milking job has been assigned to a king snake and it has been dutifully dubbed the milk snake.

King snakes, in case you did not know, achieved royalty by snacking on other snakes. A king snake can swallow a rattlesnake, poison, fangs, and all, without so much as hiccuping. But, of course, king snakes do not get much of that sort of fodder around here, because of the drastic shortage of rattlesnakes.

The most reliable herpetologist I know assures me that milk snakes dine on other local snakes. The milk snake devotes much of its youthful exuberance in running down these long slim meals. As it matures, the milk snake develops a hankering for mice and rats. Its specialty is young rodents. It leaves the running down of adult mice and rats to the black racer. For its own career, the milk snake has chosen to rummage around in stone walls, old foundations, barn floors, and the like, collecting young rodents while they are pink and tender.

July

The milk snake is a basically gray to buff snake that wears brown saddles on the back. It has a more rounded head than the copperhead whose noggin is basically triangular. The copperhead has a light, solid-colored belly, or ventral surface. The underside of the milk snake is white with black checks. So, if you roll your freshly killed snake over and see a checkerboard, you have goofed again.

Because it visits old barns, outbuildings, and stone walls, the milk snake comes in contact with man more often than most snakes. It visits those man-made sites because that's where the action is for a rodent eater.

Perhaps it would be best not to boast the next time one kills a milk snake, since the thing is harmless and dispatching it requires no skill. And, when killing a milk snake on someone else's property, one best be sneaky while in action. It could be that the owner does not share an enthusiasm about the proliferation of rats, mice and other snakes, and might take umbrage.

Aug.

Gangly, but Bluest of Blue

Of all beautiful things that gladden drab scenes, the bluest of all is the chicory blossom.

The chicory blossom almost has become the symbol of our times. At least it presides over the decay of our railroad lines. For the intense blue of chicory bobs over the edges of crushed stone or cinder ballast along every deserted railway line. It blooms everywhere in Massachusetts. No soil is too poor, no condition too difficult for this bluest of blue wildflowers. It is among those wild things that has no need of a Massachusetts Audubon Society to preserve it.

The beauty of a chicory blossom is such that horticulturists would be cultivating it for formal gardens—except for one thing. The language smith who shaped the word "grotesque" must have been looking at a chicory plant.

The gangly chicory plant with its stiff zig-zag stems grows spindly and more than a yard high. Its broken stems ooze a milky juice like the dandelion. The coarse-toothed lance leaves vaguely remind one of the dandelion.

But with fifteen to twenty two-inch blue flowers bouncing in the summer breeze from its stems, the chicory sheds rich color over wasteland. In locations where there are large colonies of chicory plants—around parking lots and the yards of industry—chicory beds splash beauty.

It's hard for New Englanders, who like their coffee straight, to believe that this blue-flowered plant ruined coffee in the Old South. In the War Between the States, the southern gentlemen who valued their coffee even more than mint juleps, found that certain sailors from Massachusetts were blockading their coffee bean sources. So they ground

up most everything at hand to make a coffee substitute. The chicory root made a fairly satisfactory brew.

Today wherever people stand up when the band plays "Dixie," you'll find the nearest coffee house serving coffee well laced with chicory. It lends what I call a slightly bitter tang. But tastes are not the same.

While chicory grows in the summer sun, blooming from July through September, its blossoms are not exactly sun-loving. Not like the black-eyed susan, for instance.

To see chicory at its best, look for it in early morning before the sun has lapped up the dew. In fact, morning is about the only time to see the blue flowers. By noon, those in direct sunlight have begun to fold for the day. In mid-afternoon, the blossoms are folded as tightly as a clenched fist.

Although close inspection reveals similarities to a dandelion blossom in the chicory flower, it appears like a blue daisy as you speed by it in motor car or rapid transit train.

August

Chicory is among those rugged flowers that get along, come what may.

The Snake Doctor

Most of us know quite well that the devil's darning needle will sew our mouths shut if we tell a lie.

Since I always was ripe for such tailoring, the inevitable presence of a green darner at the ponds where I fished as a boy was worrisome. It wasn't until some years later that I learned that the devil's darning needle was a dragonfly. All of my associates, however, were quite familiar with the creature's function, if not its name. They knew that the green darner also has less important roles in addition to silencing prevaricators. Among other things, the large dragonflies doctored snakes and stung horses. The information came from irreproachable authority, namely several generations of boys who had sat beside the same ponds and passed the word along.

To have known that the huge dragonfly (*Anax junius*) that was our green darner existed also in Asia, Pacific islands, and all of North America from Alaska to Costa Rica

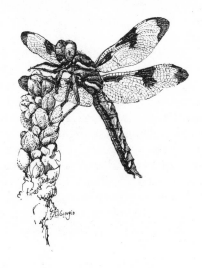

would not have impressed us. For in those days the whole world lay within a few miles of our fishing ponds—even the residents of adjoining counties were ranked as foreigners. And we never supposed we had been selected for special punishment. It would have seemed reasonable enough that green darners took equal vengeance upon those who lied in Chinese.

Our expertise on dragonflies was extensive if not scientific. We knew, for instance, that they were impossible to hit with a BB gun (they seemed to dodge the pellets), that they could not be hit with a stick, and that swinging at them with a funnel net made from an old curtain was futile.

I suppose that had Dr. Harold B. White, Harvard biochemist, wandered by our pond and told us that there are about 170 species of dragonflies in New England—well, we would have expected the green darner to sew his mouth firmly shut. But this seems to be a statement that an expert can make, for Dr. White follows dragonflies as a hobby and encounters green darners.

The one thing that we knew from observing dragonflies is that they catch mosquitoes. We saw them do it, many times. And since they hover and pounce upon mosquitoes, we called them "mosquito hawks." We did not appreciate that consuming mosquitoes is a way of life for the dragonfly at all ages. For instance, the larva of the dragonfly, which is called a nymph, swims around in ponds and devours the larvae, or wigglers, of mosquitoes.

The field of dragonfly observation lacks the excellent guide books available to birders. Dr. White says that the dragonflies of Rhode Island and Vermont have been neglected by those who survey areas to determine the distribution of species. Dragonfly investigations in Massachusetts have a long history, dating back to the mid-Nineteenth Century when Dr. Herman Hagen of Harvard was afield with net. He notes more recent Massachusetts studies by Dr. R. Heber Howe of Middlesex School and E. L. Pierson of Concord. Dr. Donald Borror has studied the dragonflies of Maine, and William Proctor did a specialized study of Mt. Desert Island. In Connecticut Philip Garma has made an extensive survey.

One learns things in unexpected ways.
I learned what "waive" meant from Rabbit Green.
Rabbit Green was a great-uncle. That was not his true
name but everybody except us knew him by that name. We
knew his true name but he did not use it by common agree-
ment. He was the first person I knew who had a dishonor-
able discharge from the U. S. Army. He joined the cavalry
to get out of the coal mine where he had begun his career
as a slate picker at about five years old. Things did not go
well with him. He had a dispute with another soldier over a
gambling debt. He settled it by sticking a knife into the
gentleman. The Army sentenced him to Angel Island, a
place later known better as Alcatraz.

With that background Rabbit Green needed a mobile
career. He became a sheep shearer. Each spring he
started deep in Mexico and worked his way up to British
Columbia, removing fleeces. No one ever asked for
credentials. He was a man without identity.

There occasionally were slack times for Rabbit Green.
He then would appeal to his sister, my grandmother, for
money. Usually the request came by letter. But one day he
was hard pressed and possibly pursued hotly. He wired,
"Wire ten dollars and waive identification."

Well, that was a big word to us rustics. Grandma gave
me a quarter and sent me to the drugstore for a dictionary.
And that's how we all learned what waive meant.

Susan, Beloved, Who Were You?

Who was Susan whose eyes were so black?

My grandmother had violet eyes. Deep violet that almost
crackled with spirit even at advanced age. But no flower
was named for her.

So, who was this Susan whose nonremembered re-
membrance splashes brilliant yellow on the autumnal
meadows of North America?

Dozens of herbals tell us that Joe Pye, honored by the
Joe-Pye-weed, was an Indian. Indeed, it is such common

knowledge that one might be wise in doubting its authenticity. But botany volumes, large or small, name the black-eyed Susan and name no further names.

One might ask: "But what about Daisy? Surely more know her name and she must have been quite a gal!" With Daisy, however, the proposition moves backward. The flower apparently first was called "day's ease." From there it tapered off to daisies. And the capital "D" Daisy was named for the flower.

But, Susie had a flower named after her!

Black-eyed Susan is among those meadow flowers that beat the Europeans to North America. She and her many sisters were natives of the American prairies and Great Plains. She has so many look-alikes among her relatives that different botanical guides assign the name black-eyed Susan to different species within the genus *Rudbeckia*.

The black-eyed Susan in bloom in August throughout New England has a remarkable record for the universality of its name. Oh, here and there across America, one may encounter a citizen who refers to the local form as brown-eyed Susan. On the Great Plains, where beef and mutton are all and romance languishes at low ebb, one may hear black-eyed Susan called "coneflower."

Even those who call her the "yellow daisy" usually know her as Susan.

If black-eyed Susan happens to be one of your favorite wild flowers, you are not alone. The great Linnaeus—the first since Adam to dispense names to the natural world— had all earth's creations to choose from in selecting a plant or animal to honor his old professor and patron, Olaf Rudbeck.

Quite naturally, Linnaeus chose the black-eyed Susan to bear the generic name "Rudbeckia." Why not? Where else could one find such dazzling color in a design of gracious simplicity?

Black-eyed Susan may seem to toss against the late summer breeze a handful of individual flowers. But each blossom exists as an intricate little village of flowers. As with all composite flowers, what appears to us as a single blossom in reality is a cluster of tiny blossoms.

The black-eyed Susan is cautious in dispensing her nectar to fickle insects. She begins courting these pollinators with her ray flowers (flowers attached to the petals) and the outer circle of flowers around her "eye." As the season progresses, she opens other bands within the "eye," and as a result the center of the blossom rises into a cone shape. Hence, the alternate name "coneflower."

Poor Guards for Hen Houses

It was our good fortune to be reared in a culture where worthy foxhounds could be purchased only from widows.

While we were unaware of it, the red fox which we pursued was as European in origin as we were. In early colonial days, gentlemen heightened the living experience around eastern shore Maryland and in Virginia by importing red foxes. There were native red foxes in North America, but they lived in Canada and penetrated the present United States no farther south than northern Maine, New Hampshire, and Vermont. Although they were red foxes, many native red foxes were black phase and wore dark coats. South of the red foxes were gray foxes, always North American natives. But gray foxes are not the running kind. If pressed they climb trees, and the fun ends quickly with a pack of hounds bellowing beneath a tree.

Of course the importers of red foxes were of the red-coated clan who ride to the hounds. But in our later culture, fox hunters lay high on a hillside and listened to the bugling of foxhounds in pursuit. We didn't need exercise, having obtained it abundantly while working in the fields. In fact, we all might have fallen promptly to sleep had it not been for the providential thinking of some honest farmer who brought along samples of his product. The product was distilled by men who recognized the federal tax on whisky as discriminatory, possibly even tyrannical.

In the days when nothing except a locomotive did sixty miles an hour, the red fox was admired for running at thirty-five. It's still impressive, since the fox makes such time without outside help—if one discounts the pressure of a dog pack at his heels.

It is an oddity that the hard running fox puts out more pad odor when excited than it does while loitering. The trait has been ascribed to a lack of predatory pressure on the fox. Ordinarily, foxes which gave off the most odor would be easiest prey for a tracker. Thus, eventually such odoriferous foxes would be eliminated from the gene pool. But it does not seem to work out that way.

The fox seems to be one of those animals that benefits from the presence of man. Recently I was in North Dakota where game managers have discovered that red foxes are taking advantage of the soil that lies between separate roadways of new interstate highways. The animals den within this slender island territory and rear their young there.

The close-knit fox families break up at summer's end. The young males, particularly, get wanderlust. Some marked male foxes have traveled more than 200 miles from their birthplace. Quite often, however, they move only a few miles. If something happens to the old man, one of the males may remain in ancestral territory and take over.

A fly book that I found beside a brook near the Grand River almost ruined my life.

A fly book now would be a rare item. It held artificial flies used in fishing for trout. Actually it held so-called wet flies which sank under water when cast, rather than dry flies that floated on the water surface. In that era, wet flies were attached to about four inches of silkworm gut which was transparent and supposedly invisible to trout. The gut ended in a loop and the angler would loop another longer section of gut between the fly and fly line, thus increasing the deception. The book was made of leather and was an accordian-pleated pouch about the size of a modern flat checkbook that fits a jacket pocket. Anglers carried their flies in the book. The one I found had about two dozen flies in it.

August

I was bait fishing in the brook for green sunfish. I removed the worm-laden hook from my fishing line and tied on a wet fly. The moment the fly sank a sunfish hit it. I was about twelve years old at the time. The next twenty years of my life were devoted to enticing fish with artificial lures. I even began studying fish as living creatures. I learned their scientific names, which seemed to change about every twenty-four months. I was becoming an aquatic naturalist. But there was no future in it.

If one wants to become a full-time professional naturalist, birds are the creatures to study. Fish may have beauty but the quality is not readily visible to all.

Sept.

A Bonus with Tomatoes

My tomato patch this year has been a disappointment. It has produced virtually nothing except tomatoes.

In a really good year, the same plants would have produced an excellent crop of sphinx moths in addition to tomatoes.

If you grow tomatoes, you probably are familiar with the sphinx moth in its infant form, known as the tomato hornworm.

This season the tomato plants in my garden have been producing a secondary crop, tiny predatory wasps whose scientific name may be in dispute. These tiny wasps inject eggs into the tomato hornworm. In a few days the eggs hatch into small voracious grubs that consume most of the hornworm's innards. They mature in from seven to fourteen days and then pop out through the hornworm's skin and spin themselves little cocoons. These look like tiny white beads. Somewhere between seventy-five and one hundred of the cocoons appear on the back of the hornworm. In three or four days the grubs inside the cocoons may become adult wasps or, if it is late in the season, pupate for the winter.

By the end of the process, the tomato hornworm which had been bright green, about three inches long, and as thick as a thumb, has become a black hulk. Or, more correctly, the hornworm's energy has been converted into wasps instead of the huge brown and black moth that would have been its more normal destiny.

The tomato hornworm, which is a close relative of the tobacco hornworm of my southern childhood, always has

September

interested me because of the effective camouflage which
protects it. One who is familiar with hornworms, usually can
find it, because the experienced searcher looks not for a
hornworm but for a folded leaf—which the hornworm
mimics. The presence of the worm is discovered in the
presence of leafless leaf stems, the leaf having been consumed by the hornworm.

In a wasp-free environment, the hornworm hatches in six
to eight days from an egg which a sphinx moth has laid on
the underside of a tomato leaf. The tiny larva munches along
for three to four weeks, growing into a fat worm with a
threatening but harmless horn on its rear end. If its luck
holds out, the hornworm burrows into the garden soil. At
several inches depth, not necessarily below the frost line
apparently, the hornworm goes to sleep for the winter and
emerges the next spring.

In my garden, either (1) the sphinx moths lay eggs on the
finest tomato plants, or (2) any plant attacked by the tomato
hornworm really thrives. It makes more sense to suppose
that the moth selects excellent plants. After all, the sphinx
moth probably was laying eggs on tomato plants for a few
million years before humans came along and started com-
menting upon the relationship.

79

Huge Black Eyes

Living close to most homes in New England is the mammal that few persons ever see, the flying squirrel.

Even when they discover a flying squirrel's nest, most persons fail to recognize it. These nests of shredded bark frequently are found in birdhouses. Any birdhouse which "was not used" during the summer, but is found crammed full of bark fibers when taken down in the autumn, may have served as a flying squirrel nest.

Usually the discovery of the nest comes as a surprise. For flying squirrels do not venture abroad during daylight. Therefore, the bird box they use appears vacant, with no daytime activity around it.

A recent windstorm blew down a martin house maintained by a neighbor in Harvard. He noticed when he picked up the house that a "mouse jumped out and ran up a tree." He took the birdhouse into his cellar and when he opened a bark-crammed compartment, three more "mice" leaped out, one escaping through the cellar door, another running

into the mouth of the family cat, and the third fleeing behind a water tank.

The one rescued from the cat and the other, soon rounded up in the cellar, proved to be not mice but young flying squirrels, about five or six weeks old and ready to leave the nest.

Although they have furry tails, flying squirrels give a flash impression of a fleeing mouse. They have black and gray fur, so mousey-colored that their scientific name translates "the flying gray mouse." But they are not mice. Neither do they fly. They are small squirrels the size of chipmunks.

The few persons who do see flying squirrels in the wild usually discover them in a window bird feeder, eating sunflower seed at night. Occasionally a flying squirrel makes a "thud" sound when landing on a bird feeder and attracts attention.

Cats and owls, both of whom are abroad at the same hours, are the flying squirrel's nemesis. In most neighborhoods in Massachusetts, New Hampshire, or Maine, the family cat can be expected to bring home at least one flying squirrel a year.

The flying squirrel has enormous black eyes, so specialized for seeing in darkness that the animals avoid any strong light.

Flying squirrels have no wings. They do not "fly," but rather glide. The squirrel has loose folds of skin along each side and anchored at the front and hind legs. It climbs trees as other squirrels do. But it also has the ability to leap from a tree, extend its legs—thus stretching the loose skin folds taut like the surface of a kite—and glide with considerable accuracy down to a bird feeder or another perch.

Before leaping, a wild flying squirrel sways its head from side to side several times, apparently taking a measurement of distance to its goal. The squirrels have been known to glide 150 feet, but the average aerial trip is 20 to 30 feet.

The last time I fired a shotgun, it was aimed at a hawk. The twelve-gauge double-barreled gun was poked out an automobile window. The driver was moving the car slowly. The hawk sat on a low limb of a tree near the road, watching us unwarily. I pulled the trigger while crouched over the gun. The recoil kicked the gun loose from my left shoulder and caused the discharge of the second barrel. The gunstock dislocated my left thumb and blackened both of my eyes. The hawk tumbled over backward from the limb.

Rather badly disorganized, I got out of the car and walked over to the bird. It lay on its back with eyes closed. I touched it with the gun muzzle but got no response. Then I leaned over and took one of its legs. The bird suddenly roused, buried its talons in my right hand, running one talon completely through. It glared defiance from its yellow eyes and dropped dead.

I never shall forget the proud belligerence of that bird. Its response to the circumstances was something that I could understand. I resolved that instant never again to shoot at something that was not shooting back.

The odd thing about this experience is that if one tells a birder about it, the birder's response usually is: What kind of hawk was it? I decided in later years that it was an immature redtail. But at the time, I had no idea of the species. I was shooting something I did not understand.

The Air Restored

Now that autumn approaches and the green plants soon will wither and trees lose their leaves, where shall we get our oxygen?

Or, to put the question the way it recently was asked, "Since green plants produce the oxygen we breathe, what keeps us from suffocating in the winter?"

There are several answers to that question—for all of which we should be thankful. But, first a brief review of the interdependence of plants and animals.

In 1772, Joseph Priestley put a sprig of mint under a clear glass vase and inverted the vase on a tray of water. He then set a mouse in the shallow tray and placed an inverted wine glass over it. A tube connected the air in the vase and the air in the glass. Instead of suffocating, as a mouse normally would under a wine glass, Priestley's mouse lived.

Priestley said, to paraphrase his report, "I have discovered at least one of the restoratives which Nature employs in restoring air. . . . It is vegetation."

With his wine glass, vase, mint, and mouse, Priestley had obtained more scientific information than we usually get today from a $10 million grant and a staff of twenty-five scientists. Still, Priestley had learned only that the air was "restored." It remained for others to learn that plants have the peculiar faculty of breaking down carbon dioxide which animals exhale and then releasing free oxygen.

Without this essential process in plants, life as we know it would disappear from the earth. The atmosphere's free oxygen soon would be bonded with carbon in carbon dioxides or carbon monoxides, either of which can destroy life.

But, what about winter? Where does our oxygen come from when the fields are brown and tree limbs bare? The first answer is that winter never is worldwide. At the time that our trees shed leaves, South America's trees unfold the new leaves of a southern hemisphere spring. Summer merely finds a new abode in its constant roving above and below the equator. And, as we are learning in an age of air pollution, streams of air travel worldwide. A whisp of oxygen from the tree in your yard may be breathed by an ox in Bombay.

The basic producer—or rather, "freer" of oxygen—exists, however, in an element that terrestrial man too seldom considers. An estimated ninety percent of the world's free oxygen is released in the oceans. The salt-water algae which exist in forms ranging from microscopic plankton to kelp blades 150 feet long are all plants. Algae make the ocean water a pleasant green or, sometimes, turn it into a disgusting red or purple. They exist as the slime on rocks and boats. Or, as the entangling weed and wrack that annoy bathers. Algae, too, separate carbon dioxide that has dissolved in water, and release free oxygen.

It seems odd that man had no inkling of the existence of

an oxygen-carbon-dioxide cycle until the time of the American Revolution. It seems odder still that in an age of outer space rocketry people find repulsive a lesser form of life upon which all life depends.

Never Twice the Same

Restless New England brooks in September bounce along on their beds, carrying a cargo of autumn-colored leaves and showing signs that they will resist to their last gurgle the icy smoothness of winter.

Of all things geological, a brook has the most attributes that humans associate with life. It has the circulation and movement characteristic of life. And it has a pulse that responds to the surge of seasons. A conduit of constant change, a brook cannot be expected to be the same thing twice.

A brook even can be civilized. But at a price. If you tame your neighborly brook, you may discover some spring that it has moved to your cellar. And, that it plainly intends spending the summer there. If you must tame a brook, have the foresight to see that it becomes friendly with your neighbor. Better yet, leave it alone.

So few of us recognize how different a brook must always be from a pond. Even water experts, whom one would suppose knew better, quite often question what harm can come from a series of dams on a brook or its big brother, a river. Dams do not harm brooks; dams destroy brooks, and usually leave nothing but trouble where brooks have been.

Among other things, dams change brooks into a series of what look like ponds. They are not true ponds, of course. The freshets of spring see to that. The passive insect, plant, and fish populations of a pond do not thrive in conditions of intermittent flood. They have chosen to live where there are no currents, and their way of life evolved to fit currentless conditions. The surge of flood water is anathema.

A brook earns a living by clinging to the land's welfare rolls. Brooks live as grasshoppers, with no thought toward tomorrow. It's easy-come, easy-go with brooks. The richness they gather today rushes spendthrift to the lowlands. A good brook laughs and gurgles as it flings away its wealth.

Ponds gather rich muck and grow luxuriant lilies and a host of water plants. Like so-called balanced aquariums, ponds generate their own oxygen supply, produce underwater jungles in which a menagerie of fish, amphibians, and insects hide. Ponds are staid, self-sufficient—sort of bankers. Ponds create their own wealth.

A brook is satisfied with the insects and leaves that fall from overhanging trees. A brook bounces above its beds and swallows oxygen from the atmosphere. Plants that intend living in a brook had better be algae or mosses and be of the sort that cling tightly to a rock. Even the insect larvae of the brook need bulldog tenacity, real holding power that nails them down to the bottom. The fish that live in the brook are mountaineers at home among the rocks. No jungle offers them hiding. After an apprenticeship of dodging into rock crevices in the bottom, they may graduate to status of the lord of an eddy. But they had better be certain they have made the grade. Otherwise, they may become the main course of the day, rather than a ruler of backwaters.

Things are different in a brook, different each day, and different from anything else.

I turned pro as a writer in the seventh grade.

Actually I had sold a few minor essays to fellow fifth graders. Those writings were conveyed with the understanding that the client would recopy the text in his or her own hand. At the seventh grade level I made a breakthrough. These more mature students were permitted to hand in typed copies. I wrote the themes and each individual's father's secretary typed them. I got five dollars, which was good money.

A few years ago there was a flurry of excitement over why Johnny can't read. Of course Johnny can't read for the same reason that he may not be able to play a violin. He has no talent for it.

September

Some day someone should launch an investigation into why Johnny can't write. An in-depth search should unearth the doings of Ms. Tillie Twitt, fifth grade teacher. She impaired Johnny's feeble comprehension of graphic composition. Ms. Twitt had no writing skills herself. Nor did she understand what went into writing. She ordered all students to write 500-word themes. And she and the students spent more time counting the words than bothering with the message. When told to write 500 words the student of average skill devotes energy in seeing how many words he can pack into a simple statement. The goal of writing is to determine how few words carry the meaning. From such beginnings things slide downhill. And the world is adequately staffed with Ms. Twitts.

Oct.

The Vine-Grown Lantern

The flickering glow from a jack-o'-lantern may be less haunting than the mystery surrounding the origin of the American gourd that holds the Halloween candle.

For there exists evidence that the pumpkin—perhaps in the same form as we know it—was grown by cliff dwellers of the Southwest as early as 1500 B.C. Yet, there are no wild pumpkins in the Americas, although a gourd that still grows wild in parts of Texas appears to be a relative.

It is not unusual that the wild ancestor of a cultivated plant is today unknown. Another, and far greater agricultural contribution of the American Indian—the maize that we know as corn—remains somewhat of a botanical mystery.

The puzzles surrounding the ancestry of corn and pumpkins, however, differ. Corn is distinctly American. The grasses from which it evolved belong in the Western Hemisphere. But the pumpkin, in some form, is international. Indeed, the true Indians who live in the subcontinent of Asia claim credit for development of the pumpkin. Perhaps, they recognize the worth of the gourd as much as John Greenleaf Whittier who wrote:

> What moistens the lip and brightens the eye?
> What calls back the past, like the rich pumpkin pie?

What indeed? Unless it be the jack-o'-lantern which calls back the days when one was young enough to tote a sculptured pumpkin on Halloween?

Before it could become jack-o'-lantern material, the pumpkin had to forsake climbing. At least its tendrils, still common to pumpkin vines, hint that it once climbed as

many gourds still do. It would seem uncomely for a hundred-pound pumpkin to be dangling from the hollow and relatively weak vines of today's pumpkins.

Since the Indians planted pumpkins in the same hills with corn, the pumpkin vine probably had become a ground runner even before domestication. The economics of cultivation would have tended to have intensified the trait. The squaws must have uprooted any pumpkin vine that indicated a preference for climbing up the corn stalks.

The common uses of pumpkins—feeding them to cattle, carving them into jack-o'-lanterns, and making them into pies (a role reserved in this age for canned pumpkin)—lead us to ignore the beauty of the fruit. Its bold yellows and oranges, both as blossom and fruit, have few rivals. The pumpkin flower, as large as a man's hand, is as lovely as any in a garden, although it would prove uncooperative as a cut flower.

Although the jack-o'-lantern dates into antiquity, the year in which the American gourd became the vessel is obscure. The idea of carrying a flame about on October 31 apparently sprang from a druid rite which involved bonfires and the ghosts of the departed. But the term "jack-o'-lantern" comes from a natural object—the pale flashes of fire sometimes noted over marshes in England, a flame possibly caused by spontaneous combustion of methane gas rising from decomposing vegetation. The English believed these same flashes occurred over graveyards. The pale flame was called jack-o'-lantern or will-o'-the-wisp.

I became a journalist because good lead pencils at the time sold for a nickel.

It happened before the start of my junior year in college. For the first two years I had followed a pre-medical course, insofar as elective subjects were possible. I studied organic and inorganic chemistry, zoology, botany, mathematics, physics, and a weird course in human health.

It was the depth of the Depression and a time for decision had arrived. My father said he thought I might be able to complete even medical school, since I was working my way. But after I completed schooling, I would need the capital to set up a practice and the finances to keep alive a couple of years while becoming established.

"I cannot afford money like that," he said. "Study journalism, and when you finish I'll guarantee you a five-cent lead pencil."

So I went to the University of Missouri Journalism School. I got a diploma there and a wife, and I never have regretted either of them. I worked fourteen years for the Kansas City Star *(with two years out as a warrior), fourteen years for the* Boston Herald, *and sixteen years as editor for the Massachusetts Audubon Society.*

Surely no physician ever spent such happy years as I have.

Prejudice and Geese

An acquaintance of mine hates Canada geese.

His goal is to wipe out the Canada goose population which breeds in New England and spends much of the winter in the region, particularly on Cape Cod.

October

To him the Canada goose is an unnatural competitor with the native wildlife of New England. He is convinced that the Canada goose never bred here under primitive conditions and that its presence now is the result of human subsidies.

I suppose the main thing that separates his attitude and mine is an age gap. I remember when Canada geese seldom bred in southern New England. I even remember when the Canada goose was relatively scarce.

Each morning and evening in autumn as I look skyward, I recognize that the would-be exterminator of the Canada goose has quite a job cut out for him. Those V's of geese flying overhead, honking joyfully—well, there's something wild and appealing to humans in all that. It is unlikely that the public would exchange willingly that warmth and emotion for the coldly scientific down-to-earth reasons that my acquaintance believes justifies squelching them.

In justice to my acquaintance, he has no argument with the Canadas that fly above New England on their way from Labrador to the Delmarva Peninsula. They are wild and in their element.

He is a biologist and his argument is that (1) Canadas do not breed here, or to the extent that they breed here, are few in number, and (2) their "unnatural" presence here causes immense winter hardship on native species with which the Canadas compete. Among the disadvantaged species are the black ducks whose winter feeding areas are dominated by the geese. His dislike for Canadas is such that although an exemplary liberal in most matters, he is a "racist" on geese, denouncing the local population for being a mix of subspecies rather than pure Atlantic Canada goose stock.

One can agree with all the observations that my acquaintance makes regarding the New England population of Canada geese. They are indeed human-oriented birds which undoubtedly would not prosper to the present extent without the help of human neighbors. They are the descendants of decoy Canada geese and of barnyard escapes, and no subspecies of Canada goose ever existed in the wild which looked like them. But what of it?

The New England Canada geese have in common with the starlings and house sparrows the ability to adapt to the changes that humans have made in the environment. Indeed, all three species thrive on those changes. Perhaps the wildlife future lies in a different direction from what purists, such as myself and my acquaintance, might desire. We can be certain of this: Whatever prospers in the immediate future will be man-oriented, because that is the species type that best fits the present New England environment.

The Non-Conforming Woodchuck

Fortunately I earn a living writing.

Therefore, I can view with exaltation the fact that most woodchucks have had a good year. Indeed, most of the rascals I know personally are quite fat. Well fitted for a winter's sleep.

If I earned a living truck farming, I might not be so glad.

October

I might find some area of agreement with the New Hampshire Legislative Woodchuck Committee of 1883 which reported at length (although perhaps with not too much accuracy) concerning woodchucks in the Granite State: "Contemporaneous with the ark, the woodchuck has not made any material progress in social science, and it is now too late to reform the wayward sinner. The average age of the woodchuck is too long to please your committee . . . ." The august group then proceeded to recommend a ten-cent bounty on the woodchuck, which was a traditional means in that era of spending the taxpayers' dollars for naught.

Not all writers have accepted the woodchuck in the same level-headed spirit that I have. Among those who maintained one morality toward most things and a totally separate standard for woodchucks was naturalist John Burroughs.

As is true of most persons, and perhaps even truer of writers, their personal lives are at times in conflict with the message they give others. Burroughs, who counselled patience, often was impatient. From his journals it would appear that he could be cantankerous despite the lovable image he always projected to visitors.

Despite his message of kindliness to all beasts, he hated groundhogs (woodchucks). He shot them regularly, and on at least one occasion tore down a stone wall so that his dogs could kill a groundhog that had outwitted them. A guest who witnessed the procedure was shocked by the unequalness of the contest and Burroughs' obvious glee. He also trapped chipmunks. These acts were in defense of his garden, as though he were a farmer who made a living growing peas, rather than a writer who profited from the wildlife that surrounded him.

The passage reminds me that the woods almost overflow with chipmunks this year. One hears them calling everywhere and they are doing an unusual amount of tree climbing—perhaps because their nasty dispositions cause them to have so many fights when they meet on the ground which they have crowded.

Anyhow, I always have wondered at the displaced values

that cause some people whose livelihood does not depend upon farming to persecute the few animals that try to live today with humans upon the acres that once were populated solely by ancestral animals.

Writing always has been a route to freedom for young persons growing up in the Missouri and Mississippi River Valleys.

From the small high school I attended, three persons who were in school with me became journalists on Chicago and Washington metropolitan newspapers. I made four. For many years whenever I picked up an eastern newspaper or switched on a radio or television set, I read or listened to the work of people whom I knew. They were from the Middle West, too. No use exhausting a list and still leaving others unlisted and disappointed. I will cite only one as an example, Walter Cronkite.

Why there are so many professional writers from one section of the nation, I do not know. I suspect that the Bible belt may have something to do with it. Many of the writers were familiar with the King James version of the Bible. There is no better instruction in writing available than the King James version. It has meter, rhythm, and style galore. The King James version came from an era during which the greatest masters of the English language flourished. It was the time of Shakespeare and a half-dozen other great playwrights. The writings of Shakespeare and the King James committee halted the rampant fluidity of the English language and stabilized it.

For those who fear that reading the King James version might harm them in other ways, let me assure them that I have seen a newspaper editor complete his daily reading of the Bible and then curse a blue streak in as colorful terms as ever.

What Is a Forest?

What is the value of a forest? This is a question that troubles modern Americans but never in the least puzzled my father. He knew that a forest was firewood, fence posts, and in unusual stands, lumber. He also considered the space that a forest occupied as land ill used. Wheat, oats, and corn were the business of land. If the soil proved marginal, then it should be grazing acres. Trees were the enemy, even at the edge of the Great Plains where trees were loath to grow. Only a lazy man permitted a tree to sprout on his land.

As for romping among trees, my old man would have been shocked by the suggestion. Even Gifford Pinchot, father of the National Forest Service, and President Theodore Roosevelt considered the federal forests as board feet and/or watershed stabilizers. The idea that the clusters of trees could shelter recreation came later. In my father's day one got one's exercise while working and for recreation rested, preferably on a divan or in a rocker.

The days in which Thoreau could stand in Concord and gaze upon Mt. Wachusett have long since gone, the victim not only of time but also of view-obscuring forests. Massachusetts and Rhode Island, both once almost entirely croplands or urban space, now have returned to sixty percent tree cover. Northern New England is even more dense. The megalopolis between Boston and Washington is fifty percent forested.

Most of us lack a clear idea of what the future of forests should be. There is, of course, a drive at the moment to harvest firewood and beat the high cost of other fuels. Yet the region was deforested by a smaller human population, so the days of prime firewood must be limited as the price, already high, inclines upward.

There are people who appreciate mature forests. They point out that few second-growth New England forests have approached maturity and that many plants which associate with a mature forest are rare.

October

Even among conservationists, however, there are many reservations regarding the trend toward mature forests. In general, wildlife thrives under disturbed conditions in forests. Wildlife prefers forest edges and the most edge exists where forest tracts are broken.

The Yale School of Forestry, always an institution that cast a commercial eye upon trees, has completed a survey of the Yankee forests to see what use might be made of the woody vegetation. The report pointed out that there is urgent need of construction lumber in New England, that there will be a dearth of fiber for pulp and paper production, that there is desperate need of firewood as an alternate fuel, and that forest industries could produce new jobs in many depressed sections of New England.

It all sounds economically viable. The only trouble is that the researchers discovered that eighty-five percent of the forests in Massachusetts and Rhode Island not only are owned privately but also occur in extremely small tracts, averaging under ten acres. So much for a massive systems approach to the local forest industry.

Nov.

Giving Spiders Work

Our annual thinning of the spider population is underway.
And what, you might ask, does that mean?

Well, it means that the nozzle on the vacuum cleaner now
penetrates corners that have been consciously neglected
since last spring. These are the corners inhabited by friendly
spiders that while away spring, summer, and fall trapping
insects unwary enough to enter the house. It may be un-
American to shun the latest pesticide nostrum on TV and let
the spiders handle the insect control job. But it is highly
effective. One must, of course, from time to time sweep
away a small pile of insect shells and wings under the webs,
using care not to sweep up the diligent spiders. But, it is
worthwhile if one likes spiders.

Sounds a little messy? It really isn't. And, I suppose one's
outlook regarding the domestic spiders may be shaped by
one's upbringing. In the period during which my voice adjusted from soprano to bass, I lived near the Mason-Dixon
line. It was a more simple period and most neat people had
housekeeper spiders as permanent guests.

The housekeeper spider was a wolf spider—a sort of
hairless tarantula that lurked in corners but occasionally
scurried across the floor. The wolf spider does not control
household pests by building web traps. Instead, it prowls
about the room like a tiger and pounces upon intruding
insects, much as big cats leap upon deer. We always had
faith that they leaped upon cockroaches and pulled them to
earth, or in this case linoleum, but I must confess never to
have witnessed such a pleasing spectacle.

Nevertheless, the housekeeper spider was a revered

member of the household. If a stranger of poor upbringing either accidentally or, dread the thought, intentionally stepped upon the housekeeper spider, it was the sort of social error that might make them less welcome in the future. Not that one expected to remain spiderless. While wolf spiders are not especially friendly toward each other—they live by the one-tiger-to-one-hill code—one could expect a replacement to arrive within a few days. But there would be a three- or four-day hiatus in which one was at the mercy of insects.

Even I find it strange that despite my communal rapport with spiders, I have learned little about the beasts. Aside from the wolf spider and the large garden spider of black-and-gold pattern, I hardly can identify a single one of the little creeps. Perhaps it is because I insist that I think of them only in utilitarian terms.

One must be firm in characterizing spiders as utilitarian, if one intends living in the same house with a woman. In my case it is especially true, since the woman was reared in North Dakota where the few available spiders spent their time spinning not webs but underwear for winter. You have to explain away spiders to someone who begins insisting around August 10 that you should stretch a clothesline from the door to the gate and avoid being trapped indoors by an unexpected early blizzard.

As a child I sat on our front porch and in the evening listened to the dynamite explosions along the Grand River as local citizens blasted for fish. The concussion killed fish and brought them floating onto the surface.

Later more sophisticated residents would string a wire chicken netting across the river and attach one end of it to the old-fashioned, hand-cranked telephone that supplied its own electrical current. Then they would crank the telephone and "ring up" a mess of fish. The electricity stunned fish and sent them to the surface.

It was an era in which the Abrahamic idea of man's dominion over all living things had reached full flower. In the Ozarks where deer still remained, although in low num-

bers, *the animals were killed by jacklighting at night. The torch would reflect in the deer's eyes and the deer killer shot between them. Wild turkeys were hunted almost to extirpation. Cottontails were shot in any month except the summer span, sort of like the missing "r" months that banned oysters.*

The game warden was some politician's nephew or uncle. His job was to arrest strangers. If the stranger was violating one of the lax game laws, the arrest seemed even more justified.

By 1937 lots of Missourians had had enough of the rampant spoils system that had ruined the state's once rich fish and wildlife resources. I was helping the disgruntled minority by stuffing leaflets under Kansas City apartment doors, urging citizens to pass a constitutional amendment that would take fish and game regulation out of the legislature and give it to an independent Missouri Conservation Commission. To the shock of us all, the citizens did that.

Living with Crows

Never ask what something is good for.

Sooner or later, an answer to that question, even though unasked, becomes apparent.

For instance, the crows in my neighborhood are valuable in keeping track of the local great horned owl. At seven to ten-day intervals, the crows either rouse the owl, or attempt to. If one is familiar with great horned owls, one appreciates the service. Despite its bulk and fierce appearance, a great horned owl perched on a high limb and snuggled against the trunk of a red pine is almost invisible. In fact, it is invisible until the crows point to it.

We shall not go into the matter of what a great horned owl is good for. The subject is crows, remember?

The value of crows became manifest again about two weeks ago as I drove along Route 2 in Charlestown, Rhode Island. The racket by three crows called my attention to the magnificent red-tailed hawk that they were assaulting.

November

Perhaps assaulting is too strong a word. They were hazing the hawk.

Undoubtedly one may take any living thing and after giving it more than cursory inspection discover that it is quite different from what it has been stereotyped. The rule applies to animals as well as humans.

In my callow youth I supposed that crows were utterly malevolent. Among other things, black was not a preferred pigment in that clime. And crows were known to be wholly detrimental to man's endeavors. Their crimes ranged from such threats to our survival as pulling young sprouts in the cornfield that was supposed to furnish our cash crop, to spiriting away baby chicks and perhaps assaulting piglets. Crows were bad. In the same period, crows were completely rural birds. They also were shot at constantly and as a result what crows we had were exceptionally wary birds.

In the southern New England environment, however, crows come off somewhat better. I am unable to credit them with hoeing corn or performing other beneficial acts to make up for their past demerits. However, our way of living has changed. We no longer raise chickens in open pens where they are vulnerable. Now I notice each spring when the crows gather in a bare but planted cornfield, they usually are searching for the eggs of killdeers. It may not be pleasant to watch a female killdeer perform a broken-wing act to distract the crow that is eating her eggs. Nor is there cheer in the crows' general attitude that as soon as they clean up all the eggs in the field, they will attend to all the killdeers that are flopping around on the ground as though their wings were broken. But the crow activity is not detrimental to man's interests. And there always are quite a few killdeers produced in the cornfield.

Possibly crows shield killdeers from the horror of conflicts and starvation that overpopulation invariably produces.

One of the things that got us Missouri citizens out campaigning for new approaches to fish and wildlife management was a new book, Game Management, *written four years earlier by a then unknown forester named Aldo Leopold.*

In essence, Leopold said that unless the environment was in good enough condition to support wildlife, there was no use stocking game because it would die. He went even farther. Although too many of us did not realize it at the time, Leopold, in effect, said that if one restored a natural environment, there was no need to stock. The wildlife would thrive and reproduce back to a healthy population. Wherever Leopold's theories have been given a fair test, they worked. Within reason, that is.

Imbued by the Leopold spirit, the Missouri Conservation Commission removed the size and catch limit on green sunfish. It also did what I considered unpardonable. It permitted hunters to kill the red fox by shotgun. Believe me, foxes were meant to be chased by musical hounds whose masters listened while drinking moonshine whisky. Shoot-

ing foxes was done only by Yankee scum. Why if my peers had a cutter dog—that is, a hound that figured out the pattern that a certain fox always ran, and then cut across the pattern to waylay the fox—well, a cutter dog was shot, period. Foxes and hounds kept their places and the fox's place was ahead.

So I wrote the chairman of the Conservation Commission that he was a fool for lifting the sunfish limit and permitting the shotgunning of foxes. He was an Old Testament Christian keenly aware of the Biblical offense I had committed by calling him a fool. He sent my note to Roy Roberts, then editor of the Kansas City Star, *and demanded that Roberts fire me.*

Always astute, Roberts sent back word to the chairman that he and I were wrangling over something that neither Roberts nor the average citizen understood or cared much about.

"If you have this Hanley interested in what you are doing," suggested Roberts, "for God's sake don't speak of firing him. Instead, educate him and maybe he will prove invaluable to you and your cause."

So in a few days I received about fifty pages of onionskin paper on the green sunfish and at least one hundred fifty pages of onionskin concerning the red and gray foxes. I read them all. The testimony convinced me that the commission was correct regarding green sunfish. And that the commissioners were damned fools regarding foxes.

But the incident served as my introduction into the world of scientific reports in the new field of wildlife management. In many ways, the commissioners and I were on the threshold of a new adventure which later would be known as wildlife ecology.

Eternal Spiny Welcome

The milkweed seed may dance like a ballerina on an autumn wind, but the burdock prefers a traveling companion.

November

The burdock is among those few plants that nature disperses by muscle power. But since no plant has muscles, burdocks and others that travel by hook or spear pick up muscle power from passing animals.

The burdock, which is much enamored of shaggy dogs, cattle, horse tails, and woolen pant legs or socks, is a relative of the thistles. But seeds that hitchhike belong to many families. They may be grasses, beans, or composites (relatives of sunflowers). Very few have flowers that would interest a florist.

While the hitchhikers have spines in common with the cacti, the spine function differs. The cacti spines repel. Cacti decorate their leaves with spears that turn away grazing animals. The spines of the hitchhikers occur on seeds rather than leaves. They welcome passers-by, indeed, join them.

By watching a dog as he lies in the kitchen chewing burdock burrs from his pelt and spitting them upon the floor, one may question whether the burdock chose the best path to survival. But the burrs do not remain in the kitchen. They are thrown out, and far from the parent plant. And not even the dog can remember how many burrs he chewed free and left behind at some other resting place.

As for efficiency, the burdock's means of seed dispersal equals any other. There are two closely related burdocks in New England. Both of them made a transatlantic crossing without the witting aid of man. The burdocks are of European origin.

Occasionally, the burdock overdoes it in the matter of hooking rides. Recently, Frederic W. Davis of Montague reported to the Massachusetts Audubon Society his discovery of a chickadee that died entangled on the spiny seeds of a burdock plant. The late E. H. Forbush reported that goldfinches in Massachusetts sometimes meet the same fate.

The use of the spear is quite common among those plants that botanists know as *Bidens* or *Coreopsis*, but which most of us would recognize only at this season, and in the form we call beggar's-ticks. Why these thin seeds that protrude from one's outdoor clothing like small brown ticks should be identified with beggars is unknown. They show such a preference for costly Scottish woolens they should be the millionaire's-ticks.

But, for some obscure reason, these autumn seeds must be beggarly in name, and thus we have beggar's-lice—which are not lice at all, but seeds that ride quite royally. Beggar's-lice cling quite unrelentingly and sidewise. They are flat, long pods that remind one of a miniature string bean that acts quite un-bean-like when one sets about dislodging them. For then they break into sections. The victim, who picked upon a beggar's-lice pod as a single unit, discovers that the seed passenger that latched on wholesale can be disposed of only at retail.

Flight from Darkness

Most of us miss that segment of the day devoted to darkness.

We block it out with automobile headlights, street lights, table lamps, and the glow of the television tube. Indeed, we keep its edges pushed back so far that to most of us darkness does not exist. Strangers from another planet might mistake us as Zoroasterists working toward the triumph of noble light over evil darkness.

There are exceptions among us who avoid succumbing to the cult of light. Most of them are butlers to the family dog, serving long apprenticeships as the end of leashes. They stumble along and when not thinking of the day's travail, marvel at the dog's perceptiveness in light so dim that it almost seems not to exist.

There are a few humans who find comfort in nocturnal strolling. Perhaps they have inherited genes from northern ancestors who became acclimated to dim light in those latitudes where winter means darkness at noon. But possibly such thoughts carry speculation too far. For the most that night strollers seem to have in common is a loathsomeness for early rising. Even if they arise at dawn, they seldom awaken before noon.

What does one do in a night stroll? Well, on a woodland path one can keep alert for owls. Not really expect to see them, mind you, but keep alert for the possibility.

It is only after dark that one may expect to see the screech owl or the long-eared owl in flight. Either is a flickering apparition cutting across the geometric pattern that winter-bare tree limbs etch against the sky. In coniferous woods, or rather at their edges, one may occasionally see the large form of the barred owl flying across an open space. Coniferous woods are not favorite walking places, however. The evergreens block out the sky glow and shelter the more inky blackness. The use of "expect" and "occasionally" in ranking the possibilities of an owl observation should not be mistaken for high probability. It may never happen. Owls fly silently and are seen only by those of concentrated attention.

One may be fairly certain of starting a cottontail rabbit, even in small brushlands near a city. And the nearer one lives to the business section of a small town, the more alert one must be toward the possibility of an unsatisfactory encounter with a skunk. Skunks are night people but with slightly urban inclinations. At any season one should have a chance at catching sight of a flying squirrel, for they not only are nocturnal but also widely distributed in New England. Yet the flying squirrel seems the mammal least likely to be seen.

A lantern or bright flashlight is necessary equipment that seldom should be used on a night walk. One should confine strolls to an area well-known in daylight. Thus experienced, one may move through a woodland with a familiarity comparative to moving about the bedroom after the lights are out. In the dark one sees things in the round, rather than in detail. Familiarity helps the brain interpret the feeble messages the eye relays concerning the contours of the path. The worst of all nocturnal walking occurs in stony or rutted areas. In daylight only the pits are shadow. At night, all is shadow and the eye reports all ruts as flat.

November

I began writing wildlife, fish, and flora essays while working for the Kansas City Star. *Much of the material came from friends working for the Missouri Conservation Commission. They were pioneers in the now commonplace field of ecology.*

In 1952 the publisher of the Boston Herald, *where I had worked two years, offered a twenty-five-dollar bonus to any staff member who submitted a good idea for a new area that the paper might cover. A friend of mine was interested in the Walt Disney nature films. The films were done excellently and attracted many fans. He suggested that the newspaper start a nature column in the Sunday edition. He said that I could write it. So my friend received twenty-five dollars, and I was assigned to an extra duty without extra reward. I continued writing the column each week through 1972 when the old* Herald *was sold to new owners.*

In 1964 the Massachusetts Audubon Society hired me to edit its publications and handle general public contacts. One of the reasons the society chose me was that a few years earlier Mrs. Ruth P. Emery, who handled telephone bird reports for the society, remarked that few white-breasted nuthatches had been seen that winter. I printed the news in a column. More than 600 persons reported to the society that they had seen a white-breasted nuthatch that season. Allen H. Morgan, then executive vice president of the society, sent invitations to join the society to the observers and more than twenty percent responded. He never forgot me.

Dec.

Builders of Stately Mansions

An unusually large number of deserted hornet mansions hang from tree limbs and from house eaves this autumn.

These are hornet nests the size of huge footballs, generally the work of a wasp known either as the white-faced or bald-faced hornet. Occasionally it is referred to in popular literature as the bare-faced hornet. Actually there are two wasps which manufacture hornets' nests. One is the native wasp known as *Vespula maculata*. The other is a European wasp, *Vessa crabro*, which is the true hornet.

All now is silence in those hulks of paper which the wasps manufactured. The workers that slaved all summer died as frost signalled an end to the temperatures that cold-blooded wasps prefer. Dead with them are the male wasps, a sex that develops almost as an afterthought. Among these insects equal rights mean that the female alone enjoys them. All hornet wasps are females until near the end of summer when the year's brief crop of males is produced.

The future of the hornets depends upon the queens produced and fertilized near summer's end. The queens have left the nest and winter in rotting logs or similar shelters. The few queens are the total legacy from among hundreds of hornets that cared for young hornets and built the huge hornet nest.

With the arrival of next spring, a hornet queen will fly to some house eave, or to a crotch among tree limbs, and build a small cellular structure that looks vaguely similar to a honeycomb. These house the eggs that begin a new summer colony of hornets. From this beginning will emerge the female workers and nurse wasps that build the shelter and care for the young.

106

December

The hornet nests are made from paper which the wasps can manufacture directly from raw plant fiber. They masticate the fiber, transforming it into a wild paper. But, the wasps also can use man-made paper in building their nests. They seem to prefer this commercial paper, particularly the better grades of cardboard. They masticate the commercial paper and shape it for nest construction.

Hornets receive a rather bad press. They usually are depicted in cartoons as swarming out the hole in the bottom of the nest and pursuing a person. It is true that hornets, like most insects or wildlife, prefer to keep people and other intruders away from their nests, which is a slightly different matter from attacking unprovoked.

Hornets are among mankind's more beneficial allies. Hornets spend their lives capturing other insects to feed their young.

In that natural history classic, *A Lot of Insects,* Frank E. Lutz tells of sitting on his front porch watching *Vespula maculata* capture flies. As he noted: "Sometimes she is mistaken and what she thinks is a fly is merely a nail-hole. Most, if not all, insects are very near-sighted."

The Breathing Rivers

At the edge of winter, rivers heave and sigh in their beds before pulling a transparent sheet of ice and a fluffy blanket of snow across their form for a long sleep.

In their writhing, rivers spread a bounty for migrating waterfowl. They drop upon the land one richness and from it gather another. It is part of an ages-old cycle that only man seems unwise enough to interrupt.

Much to his own disadvantage, man seems to have decreed that the river consists only of a trickle that wets the bottom of the stream in summer's low water. At any other season when the river does what rivers always have done, the river's action is considered abnormal.

Such an attitude could be compared only to a tailor's decision to advise the customer to exhale and from a measurement of the depressed chest fashion a jacket that fit so tightly the wearer never again could inhale. That may sound silly, but it involves the same considerations of economy that constrain rivers. After all, it is more efficient to fit the tight jacket. It involves less cloth and fewer stitches. And if the customer dies as a result, well, that's no more than what happens to rivers treated similarly.

The measurement of a river consists of both its exhaled and shrunken condition in summer and its inhaled or swollen cycle of spring and autumn. The floodplain overrun in spring is part of the river. To consider it otherwise is to court disaster. We recognize King Canute when he stood beside the restless sea. But we fail to identify the Canutes who draw a line in summer and decree that the limits of the river hold.

The swollen river sweeps from the land the dead vegetation of summer—the tree leaves, the dead wood, the fragments of corn stalks or grass. All of this detritus (dead stuff)

December

becomes food for the microscopic organisms in the river. These organisms begin the food chain that lead to fish, and from there to ospreys and snapping turtles and men. At the same time, the river spreads its enriched silt across the land, bringing to the most obscure acres the richness that man soon recognized along the river Nile.

For ducks and geese the wide river provides safety while they dabble or dive beneath its surface to pick up a bounty of food from the floodplain. It gives them living room for their brief stops at waystations between the Arctic and the Gulf.

To men who have lived with rivers, the swollen river brings tidings of a season, either spring or winter. Those who have gained wisdom from a river accept the tidings with joy.

I'm sorry I didn't think of it first. But a friend of mine who probably got it somewhere else recently told me, "Life is what happened while you were making other plans."

Tooting down Trunks

The red-breasted nuthatch goes around honking its toy tin horn as though its life were one downhill plunge without brakes.

The nuthatch's life, of course, largely is a matter of downhill. All nuthatches—and there are several types around the world—spend much of their lives upside down. They drop along tree trunks at half-inch hitches, inspecting the bark for insects. The work is done with the bird's stubby tail pointed at the sky and its pinpoint bill headed earthward.

The nuthatch style seemed weird to me, until I encountered the brown creeper for the first time. The nuthatch flies well up in a tree and works its way down. But the creeper uses the reverse strategy. The creeper flies to a point on the

December

trunk near the earth and then works its way up the tree, at half-inch hitches. Except for the possibility of blood running to the head—a situation for which evolution seems to have prepared the bird—the nuthatch style makes more sense. It obviously is easier to let one's self down by small hitches than it is to hitch one's way up a tree.

Actually neither its style nor persistent honking ever set me in pursuit of the nuthatch. Rather it is the sheer abundance of these small birds in winter. One late August when I was watching for migrating nighthawks, there were little bands of red-breasted nuthatches passing through the woods I frequent. Standing each morning surrounded by hoarfrost as I practiced cold endurance in preparation for the Christmas bird count, red-breasted nuthatches still passed through in small bands. It was a rare week in between that I failed to see two or three bands of at least eight red-breasted nuthatches.

The red-breasted nuthatch breeds in northern New Hampshire, Vermont, and Maine and occurs in extremely limited numbers in the Massachusetts hill country in summer. Its main stronghold, however, is the Canadian coniferous woods. The birds' invasions of southern New England are sporadic, with few red-breasted nuthatches present most winters.

Just as the winter finches supposedly invade southern New England during winters in which the northern cone crops are poor, so too in theory do red-breasted nuthatches. Edward Howe Forbush wrote of these birds, "A few appear in southern New England every winter as some breed here, but when the cone trees of the Northland fail to produce a crop of seeds and those of southern New England produce abundantly, we may expect a multitude of red-breasted nuthatches."

The abundant cone crop of southern New England certainly has occurred this year, particularly among white pines and several spruces.

One winter I had a red-breasted nuthatch that seemed to visit a window feeder at extremely close intervals. It was several weeks before I discovered that the frequency was caused by the presence of three nuthatches that were taking turns.

Is Holly Hex Still Potent?

Possibly you are unaware that holly will scare off mad dogs and wild beasts.

It is quite potent against witches, too. All these services of holly having been performed in Merrie Olde England, where holly was more than a Yule item. It was, in fact, a tree sacred to Druids, who were ancestors to at least a few present day WASPs.

English holly, which is related to the holly that surrounded the Mediterranean, looks like American holly but is

December

a different species. Therefore there has been some doubt, at least recently, concerning the potency of American holly in warding off nuisances. It is doubtful that a really serious test could be undertaken in the United States now, the mad-dog-wild-beast-witch business being what it is today.

Medicinally holly never has been a strong contender. So far as I can learn, the only things it ever cured were colic, measles, and whooping cough. Apparently the tree is quite effective in these fields, however, because on Cape Cod and in southeastern Massachusetts where holly grows wild, all three afflictions seem to have disappeared in this century.

I think it fair to say that holly has little use today, except as a Christmas decoration. Even this is an acquired taste. It was not until later in life that I became interested in holly. As a child, I always was far more interested in the Christmas presents.

Recently I was reading a holly journal in which a fellow who lives in Louisiana was pleading for readers to advise him of the location of holly trees whose trunk girth at shoulder-height exceeded eighty-one inches. Probably you can visualize without running out in the front yard and measuring the nearest tree that the gentleman was not looking for runts. He did, however, need to set some lower limit since Louisiana and the Gulf Coast are areas where holly trees can become respectable giants. That's where I saw my first wild hollies. I really did not associate them with snow except on Christmas cards.

The American holly (*Ilex opaca*) does grow where snow falls, but in the north it never attains hundred-foot heights. In the wild, holly reached its northernmost point in eastern Massachusetts. Some authorities gave the Neponset River as its northern bounds, but others insisted a few trees straggled into the lower Merrimack Valley. The great botanist Asa Gray chickened out in the matter, using only "eastern Massachusetts" as the limit.

If you care to see American hollies in their glory during the Yule season, visit the Ashumet Holly Reservation on Route 151 in East Falmouth on Cape Cod. It not only is a Massachusetts Audubon sanctuary, and therefore open to the public, but also it is the holly collection of the late Wilfrid Wheeler, Massachusetts' great holly man. Wheeler rescued some magnificent holly trees from abuse. He also introduced cuttings from winter-rugged Massachusetts trees into Maine and Nova Scotia.

Epilogue

Surviving Survival Training

The sharp, bitter wind of New Year's Day made one think.

What are tropical animals like men and women doing on a Watch Hill, Rhode Island beach when the temperature is below twenty degrees and the wind blowing at better than twenty-five miles an hour? Humans after all are a part of nature. By their hot African origin they are no more fitted for a New England winter beach than a palm tree.

We stood there buffeted by a wind that was cutting through a Hudson's Bay coat, a heavy sweater, a woolen shirt, and woolen underwear, making the buried skin tingle. Out on the breakwater stood a half dozen herring gulls, their webbed feet wrapped on ice coated rocks. For the gulls there will be no warming of the feet before March, perhaps April. But they can do without the heat. Their circulatory system is designed to keep the feet just above freezing. Otherwise, gulls conserve their body heat. We stood there watching about five minutes. We knew that if we were to remain much longer, our feet would have a rendezvous with pain. Our system demands that we try to keep our feet heated to 98.6 degrees, and when we falter our nerve endings demand action. We cannot, gull-like, settle for just above freezing.

My companion had experienced considerable difficulty struggling into the outer layers of winter beachwear. The delay gave the party we were to accompany a headstart of at least a quarter-mile. The problem now was to struggle through loose sand and catch up with them. The prospects indicated a two-and-a-half to three-hour exposure on the beach.

Suddenly, for the first time in my life, the thought struck me that it was not necessary to catch up with the beach party. It was not necessary to be on the beach at all. Yet, one could remember winter beach trips at lower temperatures when it was possible, nay, necessary, to lean against the wind. Such experiences are, of course, good survival training. But by now we have mastered survival. Each annual exchange of Christmas cards furnishes proof. A card here from a recent widow. A note on a card informing us that another friend has cancelled long-range plans because of a tumor that proved malignant. Another writer reports that alcohol, the common denominator of the writing trades, has hardened his liver. We have passed the short-term limits of survival.

Could it be advancing age that brought us such wisdom concerning winter beaches? Probably, but not necessarily. After all, our decision to forego the luxury of wind and ice was no more than the decision made earlier by more than 200 million fellow citizens who would not have thought of undertaking such a trek. How could one feel sad about falling into so wise and numerous a company? So, for the first time, we watched the gap between us and the beach party widen and then turned back to the parking lot.

It is our thought that time has mellowed us. Yet, we know from our own lengthy experience over the years that those who continued along the beach are certain that time marshmallowed us.